ISBN 978-0-942702-97-2

© 2018 Sandra Duncan and Jody Martin

Cover and interior design by Stacy Hawthorne and Kaitlyn Nelsen
Editing by Tina Reeble and Emily Rose
Illustrations by Kelsey Moline

Typeset in Bw Quinta Pro and Rage™ Italic Std typefaces.

This book may not be reproduced in whole or in part by any means without written permission of the publisher.

For more information about Exchange and other Exchange Press publications for directors and teachers, contact:

Exchange Press
7700 A Street
Lincoln, NE 68510
(800) 221-2864 • ExchangePress.com

Dimensions Educational Research Foundation and Exchange Press cannot be held responsible for damage, mishap, or injury incurred during the use of or because of activities in this book. Appropriate and reasonable caution and adult supervision of children involved in activities and corresponding to the age and capability of each child involved are recommended at all times. Do not leave children unattended at any time. When making choices about allowing children to touch or eat certain foods, plants, or flowers, make sure to investigate possible toxicity and consider any food allergies or sensitivities. Observe safety and caution at all times.

Bringing the Outside In

BRINGING THE
Outside In

Ideas for Creating Nature-Based Classroom Experiences for Young Children

by Sandra Duncan, EdD and Jody Martin

DEDICATION

This book is dedicated to our grandchildren who are the light of our lives and inspire us each and every day.

Honor   Hope   Liberty   Roman

Shea   Sierra   Waverly   Wyatt

ACKNOWLEDGMENTS

Bringing the Outside In would not exist without the knowledge, commitment, and creativity of others. We are grateful for your willingness to share your ideas about bringing nature into early childhood classrooms. Most of all, we are grateful for the work you do each day and the difference you are making in young children's lives.

We are not botanists, naturalists, oceanographers, environmentalists, ecologists, biologists, park rangers, or master gardeners. We are, however, proud grandmothers of eight grandchildren. For our grandchildren—and for all children—we relish their potential, encourage their curiosity, and welcome their wondrous imaginations. It is our hope that the ideas in this book for creating nature-based experiences for your early education classrooms will help you to inspire young children's sense of wonder about the natural world around them.

Sandra + Jody

PART ONE
Exploring

001 Explorer's Kit
002 Pond Jars
003 Shake a Shrub
004 Maple Sugar Tapping
005 Monarch Marvels
006 Hermit Crabitats
007 Texture Walk
008 Sand Sorting
009 Seashore Sand Inspection Center
010 Herb Hullabaloo
011 Discovering Pinecones
012 Loving Ladybugs
013 Frisky Frogs
  Recipe: Frog on a Log
014 Geckos
015 Beauty of Spiderwebs
016 Not a Stick
017 Driftwood Discoveries
018 Very Berry Berries
019 Comparing Corn
  Recipe: Corntastic Soup
020 Slug Bug B&B
021 Insect Inspectors
022 Worm Hotel
023 Aquaponics Fun
024 Adopt a Fish
025 Playing With Pumpkins & Gourds
  Recipe: Roasty Toasty Seeds
026 Treasure Tubs
027 Nature or Not?
028 Documenting Explorations
029 Displaying Nature Collections

PART TWO
Creating

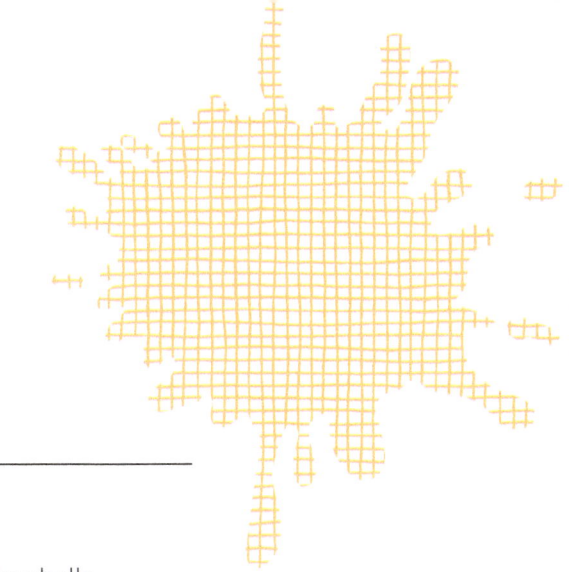

- 030 Japanese Gyotaku (Fish Painting)
- 031 Branch Weaving
- 032 Tree Cookie Weaving
- 033 Nature's Spirals
- 034 Woodblock Artistry
- 035 Twiggy Tic-Tac-Toe
- 036 Twig Easel
- 037 Sticky Sticks
- 038 Leaf Reliefs
- 039 Painted Leaves
- 040 Painted Tree Bark
- 041 Delicious Dirt
- 042 Sand Designs
- 043 Nature Artistry
- 044 Creating Mandalas
- 045 Musical Maracas
- 046 Stringing Seashells
- 047 Ok Okra!
- 048 Funny Nature Faces
- 049 Painting With Kitchen Scraps
- 050 Bird Watching Art
- 051 Milk Jug Bird Feeder
- 052 Gourd Birdhouses
- 053 Bird Nests
- *Recipe:* Whoooo's Hungry?
- 054 Papier Mache
- 055 Ceiling Tile Flower
- 056 Pretty Bricks
- 057 Wildflower Pounding
- 058 Potpourri
- 059 Wildflower Perfume
- *Recipe:* Pansy Pancakes

PART THREE
Thinking

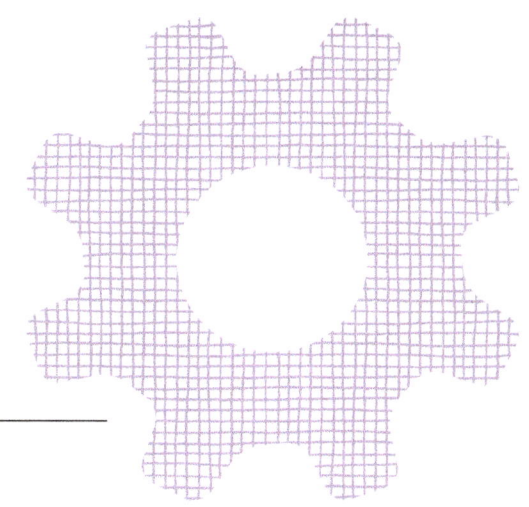

- 060 Natural Loose Parts
- 061 Sorting Bonanza
- 062 Acorn Adventure
- 063 Balancing Nature
- 064 Unit Sticks
- 065 Geometree!
- 066 Rock Collections
- 067 Rainbow Rocks
- 068 Story Stones
- **Recipe:** Stone Soup
- 069 I'm Here Today!
- 070 Alphabet Rock Game
- 071 Can You Estimate?
- 072 Writing With Nature
- 073 Using Natural Dyes for Ink
- 074 Nature Reading Nooks
- 075 Tree Cookie Constructions
- 076 Tree Cookie Countdown
- 077 Tree Cookie Alphabet & Numerals
- 078 Pound Away
- 079 Seashells by the Seashore
- **Recipe:** Seashell Clay
- 080 Alphabet Seashell Match
- 081 Seashell Journaling
- 082 Nature Construction: Building in a Big Way!
- 083 Color Swatch Nature Hunt
- **Recipe:** Rainbow Fruit Skewers

PART FOUR
Sprouting

- **084** Growing Sunny Sunflowers
- **085** Exploring Sunny Sunflowers
- **086** Cacti Curiosity
- **087** Air Plants
- **088** Fascinating Pods
- **089** Seeds Galore
  - *Recipe:* Chia Seed Pudding
- **090** Bean Mosaic
- **091** Container Gardens
- **092** Indoor Water Gardens
- **093** Natural Sponge Garden
- **094** Hydroponic Garden
- **095** Sweet Potato Vines
- **096** Kitchen Scrap Gardens
  - *Recipe:* Pineapple Upside-Down Snack
- **097** Whimsical Mushroom Fairy Garden
- **098** The Grass is Always Greener
- **099** Charming Cherry Tomato
  - *Recipe:* Cherry Tomato Jam
- **100** Farmer's Market Fun
- **101** Dandy Dandelions
  - *Recipe:* Dandelion Pancakes

FOREWORD

I never liked the notion that nature belongs in the science center when talking about bringing nature into the classroom. Nature belongs in every center. What a pleasure, then, to see how the authors of *Bringing the Outside In* provide a hands-on guide to infusing nature-based education into all areas of your classroom.

Sandra Duncan and Jody Martin understand that nature is not an end product, but rather a fundamental component to learning. They demonstrate and advocate for a nature-based approach to learning that inspires wonder, curiosity, and observation in children. The result is an extraordinary and practical handbook that allows teachers to bring nature into the classroom and into the hands and hearts of children.

Sally Fowler Haughey
Fairy Dust Teaching

INTRODUCTION

Early childhood educators have the best job in the world. Each day, we have the privilege to work with children who are filled with imagination, hope, whimsy, wonder, and delight in the world around them. Educators—especially those who work with young children—have an enormous responsibility to do everything in our power to sustain this enthusiasm for life and to assure children's life-long success and happiness.

Although it is hard to imagine, the red-headed, freckle-faced child standing before us may be the next Frank Lloyd Wright. Or, the child with the lop-sided, goofy grin, and mass of curly brown hair may find the cure for cancer. We don't know if the young child stirring rocks in a pot on the dramatic play stove will be the next Bobby Flay, the classroom helper watering the plant a famous botanist, or the child poised with pencil and paper a Nobel Laureate.

INTRODUCTION

What we do know, with great certainty, is that the possibilities are endless for young children, and it must be our commitment to encourage all of these possibilities and each child's vast potential. One avenue to accomplish this is through nature. Not only in outdoor environments, but in bringing the outside in: infusing nature-based experiences into the early childhood classroom.

Through nature, early childhood educators can inspire children's imaginations to be whatever they dream. Observing ladybugs in a temporary classroom habitat may inspire a young child to learn more about these fascinating creatures. Growing miniature container gardens might foster a love of dirt and the thrill of growth. Creating with sticks, pinecones, and clay may encourage the young artisan. Yet, infusing nature and natural elements into the early childhood classroom is not nearly enough, and is only the beginning. Equally important is the gift of time. Young children not only deserve, but need lots of time to experience, manipulate, and explore natural elements. Offer large chunks of time for open and free exploration—with each passing second, minute, and hour children will explore, discover, and learn.

Creating Nature-Based Experiences

An early childhood classroom infused with nature-based experiences offers a child-centered and intrinsically motivating place for young children. Environments filled with natural objects provide hands-on and sensory exploration that connect children of all cultures, ages, and skill levels. Nature-based experiences within the classroom promotes collaboration among children and enhances their self-esteem. These experiences also help develop children's fine and gross motor skills; integrate science, math, reading, social studies, and creative arts; and offer opportunities for children to appreciate and experience the beauty of nature.

When thinking about nature in the classroom, our thoughts might instinctively go to including natural elements in the science corner. However, all too often, we don't think beyond the science corner. The key to creating impactful experiences for natural exploration in the classroom is to infuse nature in all areas and on all surfaces. Include nature and natural elements on walls, ceilings, shelving or table tops, and the floor. Incorporate nature in all learning centers. Place gourds on the table in the home living center or include small logs, pinecones, and driftwood in the block area. Use twigs for writing tools or for paint brushes in the art center. Put seashells with holes for stringing in the manipulative area.

Be sure to include age-appropriate materials for examining and exploring natural objects such as magnifiers, prisms, balance scales, specimen containers, microscopes, tape measurers, measuring cups, and documentation tools. Provide a display space designed to showcase children's work and projects, and don't forget the most important idea: infuse elements of beauty (i.e., fresh flowers) and objects of provocation such as honeycomb or moss-covered twigs to spark children's interest in natural objects.

Inquiry-Based Learning

Although it is important to give children plenty of time to explore natural items in the classroom, it is also essential to promote inquiry-based learning. Acknowledge children's previously acquired knowledge by asking reflective questions such as "What do you know about rocks or shells?" Pose open-ended questions like "What do you think might happen?" or "What are you observing?" Give children the luxury of time to think and ponder or investigate before re-asking or posing another question. Repeat what the child says to the other children to promote confidence in self-thinking. "Sarah thinks that oranges grow on trees above ground and Thomas thinks that sand comes from crushed up rock. What do you think?" Always be aware of the importance of silence—especially on your part. Being silent and getting out of their way gives children the opportunity to come up with their own ideas and draw their own conclusions.

Equally important is giving children opportunities to reflect and converse with others about their observations and discoveries. Encourage conversations so children can articulate what they know, what they have observed, and what they are understanding in a way that is relevant and makes sense to them. When children listen and respond to conversations, they gain a different perspective about others' ideas and experiences, which is reflective thinking at its best.

INTRODUCTION

Find Nature in Unexpected Places

Nature isn't necessarily something you must drive a long way to see—it is right beneath your feet, on the playground, in the neighborhood park, beside the parking lot, or in your own backyard. You can find nature in unexpected places. Whether your classroom is located in an urban area, the suburbs, a city, or a metropolis, the potential for nature is everywhere: a dandelion peeking up from a crack in the sidewalk; buttercups growing wild next to the parking lot of the fast food restaurant; tumbling autumn leaves in the nearby park; grass clippings from a newly mowed lawn; and fallen branches from a recent windstorm. Finding and gathering natural treasures is simply a matter of alerting your brain to actively look for these beautiful and fascinating gems. Next time you are outside—stop, listen, and look around. What do you see, hear, or smell? Could anything observed around you be used in the classroom? It is your perspective, really. Open your mind to the possibilities of nature.

Experiences to Discover Nature's Authenticity

Bringing the Outside In offers ideas for extraordinary nature-based experiences designed to intrigue young children's imaginations, ignite their curiosities, and inspire the future engineer, physicist, architect, biologist, artisan, mathematician, author, or wherever their dreams may take them. This book includes many different types of nature-based experiences—some with detailed, step-by-step instructions and others with no directions. Some experiences are easy to implement, while others are more challenging.

INTRODUCTION

Although most of the experiences cost little to no money, some of them may involve a small financial investment. While many of the experiences require a minimal investment of time for you, there are others that will take time. Some require advanced preparation by you, while others invite children to gather and collect. Regardless, these projects and experiences are designed to inspire, spark an interest, and encourage educators and young children to bring the outside natural world into the early childhood classroom.

The nature-based experiences in this book are not about an end product—they are about encouraging children to use their inherent creativity and experience nature's authenticity. These experiences are not about arts and crafts (i.e., popsicle sticks, construction paper, googly eyes, and crayons), but about crafting with natural elements using our hands and imaginations. These experiences are not about learning basic concepts and achieving common core standards—although learning will absolutely happen. Rather, they're about discovery, imagination, and curiosity; conversations and collaborations with and between each other; exploring and getting to know the natural world inch-by-inch and bit-by-bit; preserving the joy of childhood; and experiencing the glorious world of nature.

Getting Started—Going Outside Before Bringing Nature Inside
Bringing the outside in requires going outside to scout, forage, and find natural objects. Here are some ideas to get you started:
- Before embarking on any experience, caution children of the

INTRODUCTION

potential hazards of interacting with nature (i.e., insect stings, poisonous berries, mushrooms, or plants).

- Just as you would conduct a safety checklist for playground hazards, you should pre-check the outdoor natural spaces children will be exploring to assure that the areas are free from any harmful objects, plants, animals, insects, or bugs.

- When experiences call for the use of tools, be sure that the tools are handled by adults or used under close adult supervision.

- When exploring the outdoors, bring children's asthma inhalers and EpiPens. Also bring a first-aid kit and some fresh water for tending to small bruises and scrapes.

When collecting natural objects to bring back to the classroom, do so with respect to the land, birds, and animals that share the Earth. Here are some additional ideas to keep in mind:

- Always be aware of the importance of conserving and preserving Mother Nature. If children pick all of the wildflowers, how will seeds develop for next year's flowers?

- Remember, nature does not belong to humans; nature belongs to the trees, flowers, and animals. This is their home so don't collect more than you need; leave lots of plants and natural objects behind for woodland critters.

INTRODUCTION

- Be courteous and remember not to collect any natural items on someone's personal property and to always receive permission prior to picking up natural objects to bring back to the classroom.

- Be careful not to touch plants, insects, or bugs unless you know they are not poisonous.

- If looking for tree bark, look around on the ground. Do not rip bark from a living tree because it may harm the tree or even cause its death.

- It is best to leave woodland critters where they are found—in their natural home. If you capture small critters and decide to bring them back to the classroom for observation, be sure to return them to the same spot you found them within a short period of time.

PART ONE
Exploring

EXPLORING

Young children love to explore the world around them, but most of all, they love to explore the world right beneath their feet, just outside the window, or right around the corner. The hidden potential in a pile of dirt or under a rock—the infinite possibilities of what a stick can become—the magic of crafting something beautiful from a natural object found on the ground—the excitement of discovering nature's secrets and how the world works—the joy of exploring just to explore.

To explore is to make a careful investigation or study, and that's just what children will do as they discover new possibilities with nature through the experiences included in this section, *Exploring*. You will learn about ways to bring the wondrous outside world into your classroom and create exhilarating opportunities for young children to explore with nature. Children will find complete joy in their explorations and develop a deepening care and connection with the natural world as they interact, question, investigate, test, define, and refine their ideas. Happy exploring!

EXPLORING

001
EXPLORER'S KIT

We all know what the world looks like through our own eyes, but do adults know what the world looks like through young children's eyes? Probably not. An adult's view of the world is from a bird's-eye perspective. Whereas, young children see the world from a myopic viewpoint based mostly on their height. Their world is right beneath their tennis shoes, and so is the natural world.

It doesn't matter if your classroom is in the city or the country, nature flits out of bushes, hops over and around grasses, and hides under rocks. There is much to be explored at the ground level.

So, hunker down and get close to the ground. Look closely and see all that you can right beneath your feet. The ground is thick with potential and possibilities for young children to discover, investigate, and explore. Encourage children's explorations of the natural world with an explorer's kit.

You will need:
- ☐ Large magnifying glass (unbreakable is best)
- ☐ Digital camera or iPhone for picture taking
- ☐ Clipboard with paper, drawing pad, or journal
- ☐ Small pair of plastic tweezers
- ☐ Pair of binoculars (authentic is best)
- ☐ Small tape or digital recorder
- ☐ Small containers for critters while examining them (be sure to release back to their natural habitat after a short visit to the classroom)
- ☐ Viewfinder for helping children focus on a particular object of interest

HINT: Making a viewfinder is easy. Find a wood picture frame and transform it into a viewfinder by removing the glass, backing, and any wires or hooks. You now have an empty frame for viewing. Picture mat boards also make great viewfinders.

Resource Guide

You Can Use a Magnifying Glass
by Wiley Blevins

Miffy's Magnifying Glass
by Dick Bruna

Look Again! by Tana Hoban

> *Teaching children about the natural world should be treated as one of the most important events in their lives.*
> **Thomas Berry**

EXPLORING

002
POND JARS

Bring the magical world of the neighborhood pond into your own classroom. Begin by taking a small group of children on a walking field trip to a nearby pond with buckets and scoops in tow. Closely supervise while you help children scoop the vegetation and water from the pond (or you can scoop while the children watch) and place in buckets. Be sure to look for plants, moss, water lilies, mud, sand, or whatever else makes up the pond environment, and put into the buckets as well. You may want to bring a wagon to help tote back the filled buckets to the classroom.

Once you are back in the classroom, place the contents of the buckets in several jars with secure lids. When the water has settled, look closely into your jars. Children will see plant life, mud, sticks, and even signs of small creatures swimming around. Document what is found in the jars by labeling, writing in a journal, or posting on a chart. Does the natural habitat change from day to day? What new discoveries might children see? Does the water change its look (i.e., clear, cloudy)? Do the children notice algae growing on the sides of the jar? Find storybooks and reference books about pond life to place near the pond jar so children can research their findings.

HINT: To keep algae from growing on the sides of the pond jar, place a quarter-size magnet on the inside of the jar and another magnet on the outside, so that the two magnets are stuck together. When algae appears on the jar's sides, making the water look green, simply move the outside magnet up and down the jar's surface, and the algae will disappear and float down to the bottom.

Resource Guide

Fish Ident-I-Cards

In My Pond by Sara Gillingham

Ocean Tails: Counting and Guessing Animal Picture Book by Gail Kisnorbo

Pond Life by George Reid

WHAT LIVES IN A POND?

MINNOWS

DRAGONFLIES

WATER BEETLES

POND SKATERS

CREEPING JENNY

FROGS

SALAMANDERS

BEAVERS

MALLARD DUCKS

PICKEREL

HORSETAILS

CATFISH

CARDINAL FLOWERS

WATERLILIES

STICKLEBACK

EXPLORING

003
SHAKE A SHRUB

When it comes to all things small and tiny, young children are fascinated. Perhaps this is so because they live in a world of giants—everything is larger, taller, and bigger than they are. So, why not give children an opportunity to explore tiny?

You will need:
- ☐ White or light-colored sheet
- ☐ Camera or phone to take pictures
- ☐ Clipboards, paper, and pencils
- ☐ Magnifying glasses
- ☐ Bag to hold found treasures
- ☐ Small containers with lids poked with holes
- ☐ Wildlife Field Guide (from your region of the United States)

Take a small group of children outside and scout around for a small tree or shrub. If you are lucky enough to have several options, it's a great learning experience to have children decide which shrub might be the best home to small critters. After spreading the sheet under the shrub's foliage, invite children to gently shake the branches.

EXPLORING

Wow! It is truly amazing to see what falls on the sheet: sticks, leaves, pods, spiders, bugs, acorns, pinecones, and a plethora of fascinating objects to explore. Encourage children to closely examine what falls from the shrub with magnifying glasses and to take a picture or make a drawing of their findings.

Extend the children's experience and critical thinking by placing the sheet under different types of trees and shrubs. Which tree had the most bugs? Were there some trees with no bugs? Which tree had the most stuff fall from it? Was there a tree with no stuff falling from it? Children could also make a book filled with images, drawings, and charts documenting their findings.

NOTE: Children may find an interesting critter to bring back to the classroom to further examine and investigate. Be sure found critters are quickly returned to their home. It is also important to carefully supervise this activity to ensure children do not touch unsafe bugs or spiders.

004
MAPLE SUGAR TAPPING

Everyone loves the sweet taste of maple syrup on French toast or pancakes, but did you ever wonder how it is made? Maple sugaring is the process of collecting sap and making it into pure maple syrup. The process is super fun to do with yummy results!

Follow these steps for maple sugaring:

1. Go exploring to find a sugar maple tree. There are other maple trees (i.e., black, red, and silver), but the sugar maple tree's sap has the highest concentration of sugar. Encourage children to find this specific tree by bringing along images of several different types of trees including the sugar maple and other varieties. The best time to find sugar maple trees is in the autumn when their leaves are bright red and yellow. Once you find a sugar maple tree, mark it with a ribbon tied around the trunk so you can find it in the spring (identifying trees is hard to do when the leaves have fallen off). A great activity for preschoolers is to create a map of the location of the maple trees. If you cannot find any maple trees, try looking for birch and walnut trees as they also produce sap, although not as sweet as maple sap.

2. Be sure the tree is healthy with no signs of injury. It must have a diameter of at least 12-inches in order to effectively tap. Larger trees with a diameter of over 21-inches can have two taps. Sap usually begins to flow when temperatures are below 32°F, which usually happens between February and March, and continues to flow for 4 to 6 weeks.

3. After selecting the tree, determine the best location for the hole you are going to drill. It works best if you drill a hole on the side of the tree that receives the greatest amount of sunshine and is just under one of the tree's largest branches. With a 5/16 or 7/16-inch drill bit, use a cordless drill to make a hole directly above a branch (a large old-fashioned crank drill also works).

4. Insert a metal spout or spile into the drilled hole by tapping gently with a hammer. The sap will immediately begin dripping from the tree once you tap it. Sap will have a thin consistency and will look like clear water. You can expect to gather between 5 to 15-gallons of sap per tap. The following year, you will need to tap the tree in a different location.

5. Screw a hook into the tree just above the drill hole. This hook is used to hang a bucket on the tree to catch the dripping sap. Place a cover over the bucket to keep the weather elements and critters out of the sap. Empty the buckets every evening and return to the tree to collect more sap.

6. Pour the sap into a storage container (plastic milk jugs work terrific) using a piece of cheesecloth to filter out any solids (i.e., pieces of bark) that might be in the sap. Store the sap at a temperature of 38°F or colder. The sap will spoil like milk if not kept cold.

7. Once the sap has been collected, use pliers to remove the tap or spile from the tree.

8. Boil the sap within a week after collecting. To make a gallon of syrup, you will need approximately 40-gallons of sap. Boil the sap over a wood fire for many hours so that the water evaporates. Once the sap is boiled down, transfer it to a smaller cooking pot, and boil again until the temperature reaches 219°F. Use a candy thermometer to check the temperature. You can also boil the sap on a kitchen stove, but be sure to boil in small amounts because the sap will generate large amounts of steam.

9. Eventually the sap will turn golden and thick. Once this happens, strain the syrup through several pieces of cheesecloth to get out any sediments or what's called "sugar sand" still present. You now have sweet, yummy syrup for your pancakes, waffles, and French toast!

EXPLORING

NOTE: Boiling sap is an adult job and should be done when children are not present.

Resource Guide

Sugaring by Jessie Hass

Sugar Snow by Laura Ingalls Wilder

Sugaring Time by Kathryn Lasky

Sugarbush Spring by Marsha Wilson Chall

tapmytrees.com
A good source for a maple tapping starter kit. It includes a lesson plan, directions, a 2-gallon aluminum bucket with lid, a spile with hook, a drill bit, cheesecloth, filter, a 12-ounce bottle with lid, and a candy thermometer.

EXPLORING

005
MONARCH MARVELS

A monarch butterfly passes by. Few adults turn to watch it. Only the small child watches the butterfly's dance as it flits among the colorful garden flowers. Unnoticed by adults, this tiny butterfly has furnished the young child with a simple pathway to fascination. Capture children's fascination in these miniature marvels by honoring the majestic monarch butterfly in your classroom.

Monarchs, well known for their intricately patterned orange and black colors, migrate thousands of miles up to the Canadian North in springtime and down to Mexico's mountains in the fall. Although monarchs can be found throughout the United States, they are most prevalent east of the Rockies and are first seen in Texas at the beginning of spring.

Look for monarchs around fields where milkweed grows as this is the only place where female monarchs lay their eggs. In addition, once the caterpillar emerges from its egg, they only eat the milkweed's leaves. So, planting milkweed, as well as flowers like May Night Salvia, sunflowers, or asters; and herbs such as chives, parsley, or dill are very advantageous to attracting monarchs. In order to live healthy lives, monarchs also need a source of water and enjoy sunbathing on large rocks in the warm morning sun.

NOTE: Milkweed can be toxic to humans (if eaten in large amounts) so planting it within reach of children might not be advisable. Instead, plant milkweed in areas that are inaccessible to children. In addition, monarchs do not have the physical mechanisms to bite or sting, but because their main diet staple is milkweed, monarchs could be poisonous to children if eaten in large amounts.

There are endless ways to bring not only the monarch, but other species of butterflies into the classroom:

- Take photos of butterflies in their natural habitat; print and display the photos in frames throughout the classroom.

- Instead of the "Red Room" or "Winnie the Pooh Room," name your classroom after a butterfly species like the "Majestic Monarch Room."

- In the spring, create a butterfly station or a space totally focused on butterflies in your classroom.

Include materials such as:
- ☐ Resource and storybooks
- ☐ YouTube videos of butterfly metamorphosis or migration
- ☐ Images of various species of butterflies downloaded from the Internet
- ☐ Journals where children can document butterfly sightings including date, time, species, size, markings on body and wings, and personal reactions or thoughts
- ☐ Posters of the butterfly's life cycle
- ☐ Art materials for drawing, sketching, or painting butterflies

Resource Guide

Bob and Otto
by Robert O. Bruel

The Very Hungry Caterpillar
by Eric Carle

Discover Butterflies!
by LuAnn Craigton

Monarch Butterfly
by Gail Gibbons

The Butterfly Book: A Kid's Guide to Attracting, Raising, and Keeping Butterflies
by Kersten Hamilton

National Geographic Readers: Caterpillar to Butterfly
by Laura Marsh

How to Raise Monarch Butterflies: A Step-by-Step Guide for Kids (How It Works)
by Carol Pasternak

Scholastic Discover More Reader Level 1: Busy Butterflies
by Gail Tuchman

butterflyworld.com

monarchwatch.org

EXPLORING

006
HERMIT CRABITATS

Having hermit crabs for classroom pets is fun and teaches children the meaning of caring for another living creature. These gregarious critters like to be in groups so be sure to have at least three hermit crabs living together. The biggest obstacle to creating healthy environments for hermit crabs is to have a relative humidity of 75% to 85%.

Here are some more tips, suggestions, and what you will need for setting up a Hermit Crabitat:

- A 10 to 20-gallon acrylic tank that easily lets in fresh air is a good size for three to four small hermit crabs.

EXPLORING

- Purchase a humidity gauge and maintain a relative humidity of 75% to 85%. Use an acrylic tank, which holds humidity more efficiently. Adding natural moss and using a spray bottle filled with fresh water to spritz on the environment helps maintain appropriate humidity levels (spritzing is a great classroom responsibility for children).

- Keep the tank at 75°F to 85°F. Placing an under-tank heater on the back of the tank is a good way to keep the environment at this optimum temperature range. Do not place the tank on a windowsill or in a sunny spot because overheating can result in the crab's death. Constant low temperatures can also do considerable harm to the crab's health.

- Selecting an appropriate substrate or bedding is important to having healthy hermit crabs. The bedding needs to be clean, attractive, and most importantly, hold up to the crab's love of tunneling. Effective bedding options include Eco Earth® and Bed-a-Beast.™ A combination of arrogate sand and coconut fibers or high quality desert sand also works. Don't forget a pooper scooper to keep the crabs' home clean.

- Hermit crabs love to climb and scamper so provide climbing toys such as rocks, seashells, driftwood, and even Lego® bricks are a great addition to the Crabitat. To help the crabs feel secure and have a place to hide, provide large shells, half of a coconut (from the pet store), pieces of bamboo, or broken ceramic pots. Adding a spider plant to the Crabitat gives the crabs an extra place to climb and hide.

- Hermit crabs demand dechlorinated fresh water, which means chlorine needs to be removed from the water in order for it to not be harmful to your crabs' health. It's simple to remove chlorine by using a general dechlorinator found at your local pet store. Dechlorinators are relatively inexpensive and come in a dropper-style bottle, so all you have to do is read the directions, and add the proper amount to the tap water. Be sure the water dish is deep enough for the crab to take a bath, but shallow enough so it can crawl back out of the dish. You could add a natural sponge or a piece of driftwood to assure the crab can get out of its drinking dish or bathtub.

- Hermit crabs are big eaters and love to consume fresh shrimp, freeze-dried krill, and blood worms. They will also eat other raw or cooked meats, fresh fruit, and peanut butter. If you want to be sure that the crabs are getting a healthy diet, you can purchase food from a pet store.

HINTS:

- When you first put the crabs in their tank, let them get used to it for a few days before you handle them. If the crabs go under the bedding for a couple of weeks, don't worry as they may be trying to molt (molting is the process of growth for a hermit crab and involves the shedding of their exoskeleton). If they do molt, let the exoskeleton stay with them as the crabs will eat it!

- Hermit crabs usually love attention so it is important to play with them. They will want to climb all over you (or the children) or walk across your hands. Sometimes when hermits feel afraid, they might pinch. Teach the children to hold their hands flat so there is less to pinch. Offer gloves to those children who may be afraid to hold the crab. Be sure to limit the crab's time outside of their Crabitat because they require lots of humidity and warmth.

EXPLORING

007
TEXTURE WALK

Young children love to take their shoes and socks off whether it be outside or inside so they will love taking a texture walk in the classroom. Place different natural items (i.e., sand, dirt, mud, leaves, grass, smooth stones, or mulch) in several shallow bins or containers with one natural item per container. Now comes the fun part! Invite children to take off their socks and shoes, and walk from bin to bin while squishing their feet and toes into the contents of the containers. Have conversations about how the natural item feels. Is it soft or hard? Warm or cold? Wet or dry? Which natural items stick to your feet? Which did not stick? Making a graph of children's responses to see which textures were most popular might be a good experience involving mathematics. Or, blindfolding the children and asking them to identify the natural items that they are stepping into could enhance critical thinking.

008
SAND SORTING

There are many types or grades of sand (i.e., smooth, rough, coarse). Visit your local landscaping company or nursery to get samples of different types of sand—about 2-quarts of each type of sand is enough (if you tell the business owners that you work with children, they may be kind enough to donate the sand). Once back in the classroom, put each grade of sand in low, flat containers and place on the floor or a table. Encourage children to feel the different textured sand and support conversations about differences in color, texture, and size.

009
SEASHORE SAND INSPECTION CENTER

There is so much to discover in playing with seashore sand and finding out what is hidden in it. If an excursion to the beach is not possible with children, bring the beach to your classroom. The next time you are at the beach, fill a couple of containers (Ziploc® bags work great) with seashore sand. Be sure to scoop in small seashells, pieces of coral, or pebbles.

Bring back to the classroom and set up a Seashore Sand Inspection Center. Although the name sounds official, setting up an inspection center is easy and doesn't take a lot of classroom space. Put the sand in small containers such as cardboard jewelry boxes or sturdy gift boxes. Place the boxes of sand on a large tray with sides to contain the sand when children explore and investigate.

Other possible items to include in the Seashore Sand Inspection Center:
- ☐ Tiny scoops
- ☐ Small magnifying glasses
- ☐ Small wire mesh strainer or sifter
- ☐ Old-fashioned flour sifter
- ☐ Clipboard, paper, pencils, and labels for documentation
- ☐ Special box for holding the exciting discoveries found in sand

HINT: Young children are fascinated by tiny stuff. Seashore sand is perfect for sifting and finding little surprises. Looking closely and finding something very, very small is an exciting adventure for children.

An old-fashioned flour sifter works perfectly for sifting seashore sand.

EXPLORING

010
HERB HULLABALOO

Many herbs are nice for smelling and good for eating. The following are a few ideas for delicious smelling and tasting with herbs:

MAKING MINT SUN TEA
To make mint sun tea (don't worry, it's not really tea), you need to first find some mint leaves. There are lots of places to find mint leaves. Maybe you find them growing in a garden—your garden, the neighbor's, grandma's, friend's, or even a fairy garden growing by the roadside. You might find mint leaves at the farmer's market or the local grocery store. Once you have gathered a handful of mint leaves, wash and put in a 2-quart bottle or pitcher. Cover the mint leaves with cold water and place outside in a sunny spot (i.e., picnic table, windowsill, or chair) for at least 24 hours. Bring the steeped mint water inside, strain, and chill in the refrigerator. For additional sweetness, add a few tablespoons of honey or granulated sugar. Once the mint tea is good and cold, enjoy the refreshing taste!

SMELLING HERBS
Fresh herbs are heavenly to smell, and each herb has a distinctive odor. Since many herbs are especially abundant in the summer and grow rapidly in gardens or flower pots, they are relatively easy to come by—either from your garden, the garden of others, or the supermarket. Easy-to-find herbs include mint, sage, rosemary, chives, and tarragon. Try putting freshly cut herbs in vases and place around the classroom. Or, have children make herb trees for the block corner by poking fresh rosemary into lumps of clay. Put fresh herbs in a bowl in the home living area or hang herbs from a string over the kitchen table low enough for children to be able to smell. Another idea is to glue fresh herbs on a piece of heavy cardboard or wood and hang up in the home living area.

CRUNCHING UP
Invite children to use a mortar and pestle to crunch up fresh herbs and add the smashed herbs to clay or playdough. For a delightful aroma, add spices into the playdough or clay such as cinnamon, mint, peppermint, almond, and lemon.

HEAVENLY HERBS IN CLAY
Playing with clay is a great way for young children to take the edge off their physical and emotional beings. Poking, pounding, pinching, and patting clay helps relieve stress in young children. Even though this form of sensory play can be very relaxing overall, what makes it even more so is giving the experience the additional sensorial element of smell. Our sense of smell is the only sense that sends information straight to the brain. Research has found that certain odors increase the ability to learn, create, and are calming to both children and adults. For example, scents like peppermint, basil, lemon, cinnamon, and rosemary help you to be more alert. Whereas, lavender, chamomile, orange, and rose make you feel more relaxed and calm.

To calm children, add a few drops of scented oils or fresh herbs to clay. Children might like to experiment with a mixture of herbs and spices to achieve a smell that is stimulating or calming to them.

EXPLORING

011
DISCOVERING PINECONES

In most areas of the United States, pinecones are easily accessible—all you have to do is go outside and look under a conifer tree and most likely you will quickly have a handful or even a bagful of pinecones. Here are some ways to discover pinecones with children:

SCAVENGER PINECONE HUNT
Conduct a pinecone scavenger hunt to see who can collect the most in a short period of time. Once found, there are many experiences you can have with children such as categorizing, classifying, and matching.

MYSTERY BAG
Children learn about size, weight, and shape by exploring natural items in a bag without looking inside. Place several pinecones of different sizes inside a medium-sized bag. Then, place a pinecone in a child's hand and ask them to reach inside the bag with the other hand to find a pinecone that is much the same size as the one you have given the child.

PINECONE PAINTING
It is great fun to paint pinecones because of all their nooks, crannies, bumps, and crevices. Once painted, the pinecones make wonderful décor for the classroom.

EXPLORING

012
LOVING LADYBUGS

There is hardly a child in the universe who doesn't have a natural fascination with ladybugs. Children love encounters with the charming ladybug and its cheery polka-dotted back, but sometimes, visits from the ladybug can be few and far between.

Here is how to encourage ladybugs to visit your outside area:

- Include bushes and plants on the playground or near the classroom window that ladybugs like to visit such as angelica, marigold, and cosmos. Herbs like dill, fennel, and caraway are also helpful in attracting ladybugs.

- Spray the plants and bushes with "Ladybug Perfume," which is a mixture of 10 cups water, 1 cup sugar, and 1 cup whey yeast or brewer's yeast.

- Make ladybug feeders. Here are two kinds of easy-to-make feeders:

BAMBOO LADYBUG FEEDER
Simply purchase or find a piece of bamboo. If you don't have bamboo growing in your backyard, you can find bamboo sticks at a garden center, home improvement, or craft store. For one feeder, you will need about 12 pieces of bamboo that are approximately 15-inches long and 3 or 4-inches in diameter. Cut the bamboo to the desired length. With sandpaper, smooth any rough edges created by the saw (adult job).

To help ladybugs enter the feeder, cut each end of the bamboo at a slight angle. Drill several ½-inch holes in the bamboo including a hole at each end. Thread a 3-foot piece of twine in both holes at the end of the bamboo, then tie the two twine ends together with a double knot. Bait the feeder with two or three raisins and hang the feeder on a fence, in a tree, or on a bush.

WOOD DRAWER LADYBUG FEEDER
Find a small wood drawer to use as the base for the feeder. The drawer doesn't have to be in pristine condition because it will be placed outside. Places to look for old drawers are resale shops, garage or yard sales, or in the basement. Asking parents for donations is another way to secure wood drawers.

Obtain bamboo sticks that have small diameters about ½ to 1-inch. Cut the sticks into lengths of approximately 6-inches. The sticks do not have to be all exact lengths and diameters. Fill the drawer with bamboo sticks, and glue each stick to the drawer's bottom. If you are going to hang the feeder, attach a wire or piece of twine to the back of the drawer for easy hanging. Bait the feeder with a few raisins to attract lady bugs to their new home.

If you are unable to attract ladybugs to your playground, garden, or window sill, try these two ideas to give children the magical experience of ladybugs:

- Purchase live ladybugs on the Internet. After a few days in captivity, it is important to discuss with the children where the ladybugs are happiest, which is in the wild. Be sure to release the ladybugs into their natural surroundings. It is best to release ladybugs at dusk so they will stay put where you released them. Since ladybugs ravenously consume aphids, look for pests on your plants before releasing. The ladybugs will want to stay in the neighborhood if they have something to dine on!

NOTE: Some ladybugs (i.e., Asian Lady Beetle) bite. Although their bite is non-poisonous, and will not inflict harm, it is best to buy the red-backed ladybug with seven spots: one spot directly behind the head and three spots on each side of the head.

- Visit a garden center. You can find ladybugs hanging out at most garden stores. Check the Internet for times of the year when ladybugs are most active in your neck of the woods. To give the children the opportunity to see a real ladybug up close, hold

EXPLORING

or place a damp sponge nearby a plant they are visiting. Invite children to examine their little ladybug friends to discover how many legs they have, how many spots, where the antennae are located, and discover how their wings work. Bring along magnifying glasses, bug viewers, and photos of ladybugs for visual comparison. Take photos of ladybugs to bring back to the classroom and document or graph how many of the observed ladybugs had more than two, four, or six spots; how many spread their wings; and any other observations the children made. Continue children's ladybug explorations with these additional ideas:

LADYBUG COUNTING CARDS

Make ladybug-shaped cards with the numbers one through ten on the front side of each card. On the backside of the cards, create black dots (or spots) that represent the number on the front. Offer loose parts such as buttons, glass beads, pom-poms, stones, or pumpkin seeds. Invite children to place the correct number of objects for each number on the card's front side. For self-checking, remove the objects from the ladybug card and flip it over to see if the loose objects match the number of dots. This is a good one-to-one correspondence activity, which is a pre-math skill.

LADYBUG SNACKS

Why not encourage children to eat healthy snacks by creating ladybug snacks? Not only will they like making the ladybug snacks, but they will really enjoy eating them!

Try out these four ideas for making ladybug snacks:

- Ritz-type crackers covered with cream cheese and a few dried cherries.
- Vanilla wafers spread with yogurt and raisins.
- Whole wheat bread circle covered with soy butter, and a few pomegranate seeds or dried blueberries.
- Cherry tomato half (body) and black olives (head and spots) stuck together with cream cheese.

Resource Guide

Are You a Ladybug? by Judy Allen

The Grouchy Ladybug by Eric Carle

Ten Little Ladybugs by Melanie Gerth

It's a Good Thing There Are Ladybugs by Joanne Mattern

Lady Bug (Life Cycles) by David M. Schwartz

Little red bug, oh so cute, Here's a black spot for your suit...
Susan M. Paprocki

EXPLORING

013
FRISKY FROGS

Frogs make easy-to-handle classroom pets, and with the proper care, they can live a long time (15 years). Instead of capturing wild frogs, make sure to purchase frogs from a pet or fish store that are captive bred, free of disease, and are not poisonous.

Here's some more tips for happy frogs in the classroom:

- Select the right size. Smaller frogs are active, so they are more intriguing and interesting for young children to observe.
- The majority of frogs have simple lifestyles and comfort needs (i.e., light, temperature, humidity). Frogs are, however, sensitive to contaminants in their environment so their home needs to be kept clean. Assure the frogs' well-being by using the right tank. A half land/half water environment is one of the most common types of tank needed for frogs. Some frogs hibernate, so be sure to provide the appropriate environment conditions for hibernation.
- Reptomin Food Stick is an inexpensive food source for frogs and can be found at most pet or fish stores.

RECIPE
Frog on a Log

Here's what you need for each frog on a log:

- ☐ 1 celery stick (log)
- ☐ 1 tablespoon cream cheese (log filling)
- ☐ 4 raisins, sliced green olives, or green grapes (frogs)

Invite children to spread the cream cheese on the celery stick and place the frogs on the log!

EXPLORING

014
GECKOS

Geckos make nice classroom pets. There are over 2,000 different species found around the world and they come in lots of different colors and patterns. You could say that Geckos are as individual as the children in your classroom. Most Geckos are nocturnal, so they may sleep a lot during the day and be active at night. They make noises and may even chirp or bark. There is also a "day version" of the Gecko that is more likely to be awake during the day.

The most common Gecko to keep as a classroom pet is the Leopard Gecko because they are gentle and easy to maintain. Although the Leopard Gecko is one of the easiest lizards to have in the classroom, it is still important to prepare an appropriate and comfortable habitat for the lizard. Geckos are most comfortable in a glass tank or terrarium that is long, shallow, and has about 10-gallons of water per Gecko. Be sure the tank has a wire mesh lid to allow for natural light and fresh ventilation. Place a substrate (i.e., paper towel, newspaper, or artificial turf) on the bottom of the tank so it can be easily cleaned and replaced. Include some plants and landscaping in the tank. Use real or artificial plants along with some natural moss, which should be kept moist and damp. Include rocks, sticks, pine boughs, or driftwood so your Gecko can climb and exercise.

A small piece of natural bamboo makes a perfect, safe spot for a timid Gecko.

Because Geckos are desert critters, they need a warm home of 85°F to 90°F. If a black heat lamp is used, keep it on for 14 hours of light during the summer and 12 hours during the winter. Automatic timers help regulate the appropriate light and dark time periods. A hygrometer helps regulate the tank's humidity to 40% or lower. Don't forget to supply small, shallow bowls for water and the Gecko's favorite foods: ants, crickets, beetles, roaches, moths, and flies.

Check with your local pet store or the Internet for additional information on how to keep Geckos healthy and happy in the early childhood classroom. Prepare to get attached because your Gecko could live up to 10 years!

Children see magic because they look for it.
Christopher Moore

015
BEAUTY OF SPIDERWEBS

In our busy lives filled with plastic, technology, and man-made products, spiderwebs are often considered a nuisance and perhaps a safety issue—especially when found in the classroom. We have a tendency to quickly brush webs away from the classroom corners or beneath shelving units, and we become annoyed when the web reappears the next morning. Rarely do we take a close look at the incredible detail and beauty of a typical spiderweb; think about why the spider rebuilds its web day after day; or consider how the spider knows or learned to build a web in the first place. The following are several experiences to help you take in the wonder of a spiderweb and share your discoveries with the young children in your classroom.

SPIDERWEB RELIEFS

If there are no spiderwebs in your classroom, take children outdoors and begin looking for one. You might be surprised at how easily webs can be found, especially in the early morning dew when the sunlight is low. Prior to going on a spiderweb hunt with children, do a preliminary walk around the neighborhood to look for spiderweb locations in case the children come up empty-handed. Look on low tree branches or bushes, in flower cups, on gates or streetlights, low in the grass, or on sidewalk lamps. Also, prior to the hunt, be sure to talk to children about safety by stressing the importance of not touching or picking up a spider if they happen to see one.

Bring along some pieces of black paper and a spray adhesive. Encourage children to find a deserted spider web. Spray the web with the spray adhesive, lay a piece of black paper on top, and gently lift. When dry, spray the web with a gloss finish, which will highlight the design of the web and help to keep it intact. Children will enjoy looking at the beauty of the spiderwebs and observing the many differences between them in terms of size, pattern, and intricacy. Spiderwebs are fascinating to children because they are keenly interested in observing the intricacy of the web and the way in which the spider spins a web. Check out the Internet for time-lapse videos of spiders making webs to show to the children.

SPIDERWEB MAZE

If you have a hallway available in or near your classroom, use it to make a spiderweb maze. Hang black crepe paper streamers in a crisscross fashion to look like a spiderweb. Encourage children to wiggle their way through the maze without breaking or pulling the streamers down. Illustrate how to crawl under or lift their legs over the web to reach the other side. If you do not have a hallway, you can tape a spiderweb design on the floor and encourage children to step into the various web sections without stepping on the tape. Place cardboard insects in certain sections of the web and have children bend over on one foot and pick up the insect—just like a spider catches insects!

SPIDERWEB TOSS

To help children understand how a spider catches its prey for nourishment, make a game out of it by adhering painter's tape in a webbed fashion to the classroom door opening (sticky side facing inside the classroom). Invite children to wad up small pieces of paper to make paper balls to throw into the web. Unless the balls go through the web's openings, they should stick to the tape much like an insect sticks to the spiderweb. Perhaps an objective could be to get through the spiderweb and not get caught for lunch!

Resource Guide

Insects, Spiders and Worms: Children's Science & Nature by Baby Professor

Spiders by Gail Gibbons

National Geographic Readers: Spiders by Laura Marsh

EXPLORING

016
NOT A STICK

It may look like just an ordinary twig or stick, but this little gem of nature can be so much more. What young child doesn't like to pick up sticks, carry them all around, and mess about with them? Children and sticks are like two peas in a pod. Playing with sticks is almost an inborn action—a natural inclination, a built-in magnet, and attraction. So, why not take sticks and use them in a purposeful way in the classroom?

With sticks, children can:
- Build structures.
- Compare and contrast.
- Line up according to length.
- Classify according to weight.
- Transform into a fairy or magician with a magical wand.
- Categorize by color, texture, and even smell.
- Be an accessory to scientific inquiry.
- Weave and decorate.
- Change into a tap-tap-tap music maker.
- Turn into a storyline prop.
- Use as a writing utensil, paintbrush, or pointer.
- Become a construction tool for architects in the block area.

So you see, a stick is not just a stick, but a whole lot more. A stick is whatever and wherever children's imaginations take it—the possibilities are infinite and boundless!

EXPLORING

017
DRIFTWOOD DISCOVERIES

Driftwood are pieces of wood that have been washed onto the shore or beach of a lake, ocean, or river by the water's natural movement. They are considered debris by some, but can actually be very important as they provide shelter for birds, plants, and other little critters. They can also be collected and become an important and useful natural element in the classroom.

The following are some ideas for incorporating driftwood into your classroom:

- Add driftwood to the block area for children to use while building, stacking, and connecting other blocks.

- Use driftwood as a canvas for art projects such as pencil drawings, acrylic painting, or block printing.

- Include driftwood in the science area for comparing, contrasting, weighing, and documenting children's observations.

- Driftwood can become a tool for stirring, a pillow for a baby doll, or an ingredient for the pretend stew in the home living area.

- In the tinkering area, children can create beautiful sculptures and mobiles with pieces of driftwood, thin wire, pieces of twine and yarn, wood glue, and loose parts such as sea glass, tiny seashells, and miniature pinecones.

EXPLORING

018
VERY BERRY BERRIES

There are so many delicious berries for young children to discover such as blackberries, strawberries, blueberries, and raspberries.

The following are several ideas to introduce children to the wonderful world of berries:

- Go berry picking at a local farm or berry patch.

- Visit a farmer's market to see seasonal berries on display.

- Take an excursion to the neighborhood grocery store and visit the produce section.

- Place a bowl of berries in the art center along with watercolors and paper; encourage children to paint a picture of the berries in the berry bowl.

- Take pictures of berries with your phone, download, and print out. Frame the images and place in the home living area of your classroom.

- Find non-fiction books or storybooks about berries for children to read in your classroom.

- Have a berry tasting party and invite children to compare and contrast the different berries. Ask questions like: What are their colors? Which ones are smooth? Which ones are bumpy? Have they enjoyed berries in another way such as jam, in a pie, or in ice cream? What kind of seeds can you see on the outside and the inside of each berry? Which are sweet and sour? Consider creating a graph of their discoveries or the children's likes and dislikes of the different berries.

- Make a berry kabob by spearing berries on a toothpick. Eat and enjoy!

- Make a very berry milkshake.

Here's what you need:
- ☐ A handful of fresh berries (frozen berries also work, but use a spoon!)
- ☐ 2 cups of milk (white, almond, banana, or soy)
- ☐ A handful of ice

Don't worry about exact proportions—almost any combination of milk, berries, and ice will work. Add a little cinnamon, nutmeg, or vanilla extract for an extra special tasting treat. Instead of milk, try yogurt or even ice cream, which is sure to be a winner!

EXPLORING

019
COMPARING CORN

Arrange a variety of corn (i.e., dried, white, yellow, peaches and cream, and sweet) out on a table for children to see and touch. Provide magnifying glasses to see small details of the corn. Include other items of interest on the exhibit table such as cornstalks, cornhusks, popcorn kernels, popped corn, canned corn, cornmeal, corn flakes, and corn chips.

Be sure children understand these items are for seeing, and tasting of these different types of corn will be done at another time. Ask the children which types of corn they have tried before and make a chart of their responses. Ask them which type they would like to try at snack time. Enjoy as many varieties as you can provide.

An extension of this activity is to place Indian or popcorn in the classroom's sensory table and encourage children to take the kernels off of the ears of corn. The hard corn kernels placed inside medicine bottles, paper towel tubes, or plastic bowls with lids make terrific music and noise makers!

DIFFERENT TYPES OF CORN

YELLOW	DRIED	FLOUR
PEACHES & CREAM	SWEET	DENT
WHITE	INDIAN	FIELD
BLUE	FLINT	POD
MULTI-COLORED	POPCORN	WAXY

RECIPE
Corntastic Soup

Children usually love anything they have made and created with their own hands, so making corn soup with their assistance is an easy way to introduce this wonderful vegetable into children's eating repertoire.

You will need:

- ☐ 2 cans of Cream of Chicken soup
- ☐ 2 cups of water
- ☐ 1 package of frozen corn (or 2 cups fresh corn)
- ☐ Sour cream
- ☐ Shredded cheddar cheese
- ☐ Salt & pepper (to taste)
- ☐ Crockpot

Give children opportunities to measure, spoon, and pour the soup's ingredients into a cold crockpot. Let the soup cook for 2 to 4 hours, or just until it is warmed up. Have children spoon out sour cream or grate cheddar cheese to put on top of the soup. Enjoy!

EXPLORING

020
SLUG BUG B&B

Although these adorable little slug bugs are slimy and slow, they are very interesting creatures. Actually, slugs are not bugs, but soft-bodied mollusks or snails without their shell house. Slugs play an important role in the natural ecosystem because they remove decaying plant matter and are an important food for some animals. Slugs can be found in heavily wooded, moist areas such as under leaves or logs. Much to a gardener's chagrin, slugs can also be found in the garden happily munching on vegetable leaves.

Slugs emerge at night to feed on leaves, sprouts, or decaying vegetation. Because slugs like it when it's cooler, you can usually find them more readily in the spring and fall. Baby slugs are very tiny, but can grow to be as large as 10-inches in length, and when they want to fit into tiny holes, they can flatten and make themselves 20 times longer than their normal bodies. Slugs might be yellow, grey, brown, or black in color.

Although making a comfortable habitat is pretty simple, it is important to think of the habitat as a temporary place for them to stay—like a B&B. Slugs are happy to stay for a while, but there's no place like home, so be sure to return the slugs to the wild after a few vacation days in the classroom (if you found the slugs in a garden, the gardener would most likely appreciate the slugs being returned elsewhere). Slugs can live up to 6 years in the wild, but not nearly as long in a man-made habitat.

Follow these steps to make your own Slug Bug B&B:

1. Since the slugs are just passing through, the Slug Bug B&B doesn't have to be elaborate. A gallon pickle jar or bulk food plastic jar with a tight-fitting lid works just fine (ask the center's cook or nearby restaurant for an appropriate container).

2. Poke some very tiny holes in the lid for ventilation and lay the jar on its side.

3. Add some moist dirt on the bottom of the container along with grass, leaves, twigs or bark, and a few small rocks. Voilá—a four-star B&B for slug bugs!

HINT: Slugs can climb in and out of places fairly easily. Make sure the lid holes are small enough that they don't escape into the classroom. For a great B&B breakfast, add small amounts of lettuce leaves, carrot peels, and potato skins.

Resource Guide

Some Smug Slug
by Pamela Duncan Edwards

The Little Book of Slugs
by Allan Shepherd and Suzanne Galant

Slugs in Love
by Susan Pearson

Mr. Slug's Breakfast
by Sandra L. Wirfel

EXPLORING

021
INSECT INSPECTORS

Children live in the here and now. They are truly interested in what is right below their feet and love to hunt for little creatures outdoors. For young children, it doesn't matter whether these creatures are flying or crawling, fuzzy or hard, wings or antennas, colorful or dull, something magical happens when children meet insects or bugs.

Encourage children to be gentle with their new insect friend. If they bring the insect inside for further inspection, teach respect for the natural world by finding a safe space (small clear container with hole-poked lid) for the insect's short visit, and make sure the insect is quickly returned to its natural home.

Prior to returning the insect to the wild, take a few pictures with your phone or camera to capture the moment and keep the visitor's image fresh in the children's minds. Print out the image of the insect, frame the picture, and place it in the science area. Once the insect has been returned to its natural home, extend children's natural curiosities by finding resource books, storybooks, and images of the same species.

EXPLORING

022
WORM HOTEL

A worm might be the easiest pet you will ever have in the classroom. You don't often see worms because they live underground and that's the way they like it! So, if you want to keep worms in your classroom, you will need a large container or worm hotel. Glass or acrylic containers allow children to see the worms' activities including the tunnels they build. It is best to just observe worms because it could hurt them to be held. If you have to move the worm, pick it up with some soil around it and transfer to another home.

Because worms live underground, they really do not like the sun. Worms can even get a sunburn, dry out, and die. Be sure to dampen the soil, but do not soak it, as worms do not like to be too wet.

Worms need food to eat. Typically, they eat kitchen scraps and excrete a dirt-like substance that is very nutritious for plants growing in the worm hotel. Organic scraps such as potato peels, apple skins, and carrot peels are particularly yummy for worms. Invite children to peel these vegetables and feed the peel scraps to the worms. Remember, worms are actually wild animals and prefer to be outside. They will live much longer and be healthier if you only spend a short time with them. Think of worms as classroom visitors staying in the worm hotel for a short time before they move on, and go home.

EXPLORING

023
AQUAPONICS FUN

Aquaponics is the art of raising fish to fertilize plants that will clean the water and re-circulate it back to the fish. This environmentally friendly process uses 90% less water than a potted plant, and no chemicals or pesticides are needed. By using aquaponics in the classroom, young children learn how to grow food and care for living things. To create a mini-aquaponics system, all you need is a mason jar and a plant pot to insert into the jar. A disposable plastic drinking cup works perfectly as the plant pot, which is inserted into the opening of the mason jar or other selected container.

There are a variety of creatures that can live in a mason jar aquaponics. For example, a Betta fish lives comfortably in a gallon-size jar. If a smaller jar is used, a ghost shrimp, Assassin Snail, or Endlers work perfectly. If you use Endlers for your aquaponics, include a male and female as they breed very quickly, and you will soon have plenty of creatures living in your jar.

Choose a plant to grow in the jar. Herbs like basil and parsley or leafy greens like kale and spinach work really well (start out by growing the plant in soil so you will have roots or you can buy a plant with the roots attached). Clean the roots of the plant as much as you can before positioning in the aquaponics system. Just one plant can clean and offer a hiding place for your creature.

Add some growth medium such as small pieces of gravel to the bottom of the jar. Before you add water to the jar, let it sit for several days and add a little Vitamin C to reduce the chloramines. Next, you are ready to add a pot to the jar opening. Place gravel in the pot or a disposable plastic cup and then add your plant. Poke a hole in the bottom of the pot or cup to allow water and air to pass through to the plant roots. Other accessories such as a light or heater could be used as well.

Resource Guide

theaquaponicsource.com

A great online resource for additional ideas on both establishing and maintaining aquaponics systems.

024
ADOPT A FISH

There are several ways to raise children's environmental awareness including caring for a plant, looking at insects, reading books about nature, or maybe even welcoming a fish into the classroom. Whatever you do, be sure to allow plenty of time for conversation, using children's reactions, comments, and questions as the foundation for what to do next.

For example, in bringing a fish into the classroom, children may have lots of questions about how the fish eats, breathes, poops, or sleeps. All this conversation leads to thoughts about how much we feed the fish and how to clean his home. We may not always know the answers, but with today's quick access to the Internet, the answers are readily nearby. Ultimately, children can begin to understand in the simplest of ways about a fishbowl ecosystem: land, water, air, and pollution.

025
PLAYING WITH PUMPKINS & GOURDS

Visit a farmer's market or pumpkin farm and come away with three different sizes of the same gourd or pumpkin. Encourage children to measure the height, circumference, and bottom using a tape measure, and record the measurements on a chart.

Here are two additional challenges:

- Ask children to predict the buoyancy of each gourd or pumpkin. Discuss the word buoyancy and then provide a bucketful of water. Ask the children if they think the gourd or pumpkin will float to the top or sink to the bottom of the water.

- Use a bathroom or old-fashioned scale to weigh the gourd or pumpkin. Record their measurements on a chart and promote conversations about comparing the differences in measurements and weights between the three sizes of the gourd or pumpkin.

POUNDING PUMPKINS
Pumpkins, gourds, and squash make terrific pounding surfaces. Once the gourd has a sufficient number of holes in it, take to the garden or nearby forest for wood lawn creatures to enjoy.

PUMPKIN PARTY
Children can engage in a multi-faceted sensory exploration of the pumpkin's insides. Scoop the "guts" from three to four large pumpkins and place in a shallow storage bin. Invite children to explore the ooey gooey seeds, fibrous strands, and pulp with their fingers or even their toes! Provide items such as measuring cups, mashers, and spoons to continue their discoveries.

MINI PUMPKIN PRINTS
Cut mini pumpkins in half and clean out their insides. Squirt several different colors of paint onto paper plates or tins. Encourage children to use their mini pumpkin as a stamp or a brush to make colorful prints.

RECIPE
Roasty Toasty Seeds

After your pumpkin explorations don't throw away the seeds! Continue the fun by roasting pumpkin seeds for a delicious and healthy snack.

You will need:

- 1½ cups pumpkin seeds
- 2 tablespoons melted butter or olive oil
- 2 teaspoons salt

1. Preheat the oven to 300°F.

2. Scoop out the inside of your pumpkin.

3. Separate the pumpkin seeds from the pulp. It is ok to leave some pulp on the pumpkin seeds because it adds flavor. Just remove the biggest pieces.

4. Toss the pumpkin seeds in a bowl with the melted butter or olive oil. Add salt and toss.

5. Spread the pumpkin seeds in a single layer on a baking sheet.

6. Bake for 45 minutes, or until the pumpkin seeds are golden brown. Stir the pumpkin seeds occasionally while they're baking so that they toast evenly.

Include gourds and pumpkins in the home living area for dramatic and authentic play.

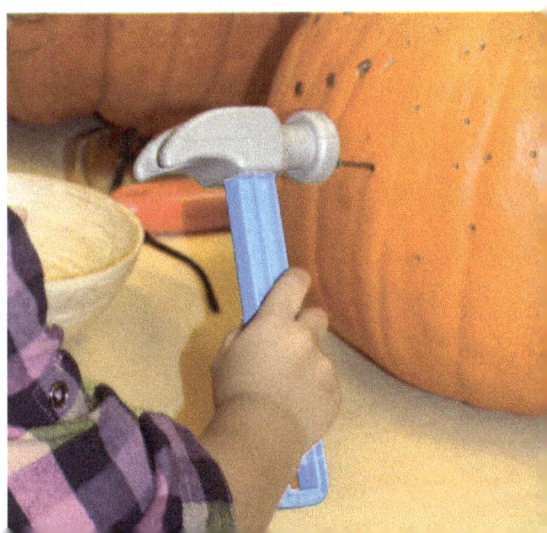

EXPLORING

026
TREASURE TUBS

Create sensory-rich nature experiences with treasure tubs. Sensory experiences are critically important to children's growth and development. Treasure tubs give children opportunities for discovery and investigation of the natural world—right in the middle of your classroom. The best part? Nature is free and readily available—all you have to do is go outside and collect nature's treasures!

The treasure tub idea is simple: Find a container (large or small), fill it with natural objects (many or few), put the tub filled with enticing treasures on the floor, and watch the exploration begin!

Here are some additional tips for creating treasure tubs:

- For younger children, select a smaller-sized tub for easier handling.
- Select a tub that is deep enough to hold larger objects, but not so deep that it is difficult for the smaller child to find and retrieve the stuff in the tub.
- Be sure the tub is sturdy and able to hold up to busy hands and bodies.
- For convenience in storing, select a tub with a cover.
- Clear tubs allow children to see what is inside before they open it.
- Choose tubs with handles for easy transporting by children.
- Smaller hands require smaller objects for handling ease (always be aware of choking hazards).
- Change the tub's contents when children's interest wanes.
- Only objects from nature are placed in the tub—no man-made, synthetic, or commercially purchased objects.

EXPLORING

027
NATURE OR NOT?

Gather a variety of objects that are plastic or pretend, and some natural elements such as a stick, seashell, and palm leaf. Place these objects on a table so children can see the items that will be buried out of sight. Give children an opportunity to see and discuss the objects. Have a conversation about what is real and what is not—what is nature and what is man-made. After the conversation, bury the objects in the sensory/sand table or in a plastic container filled with sand.

As the children dig and find an item, discuss which items are natural and which are man-made. Some may be confusing such as the plastic insect. Children may automatically think it is a natural element because insects are a form of nature, but obviously, it is pretend and man-made. Invite children to place the found items in separate bins or buckets designating whether they are nature (real) or man-made (pretend).

MAN-MADE (PRETEND)	NATURE (REAL)
PLASTIC TOY CAR	PINECONE
CRAYON	STICK
PLASTIC FLOWER	ROCK
COMB	SEASHELL
BALL	FLOWER

EXPLORING

028
DOCUMENTING EXPLORATIONS

Playing outside is a high-ranking activity for young children. Playing outside in a natural environment is even better. Encourage children to capture these outdoor experiences and discoveries in nature by using a camera. Children love to play with gadgets, so learning how to use a real-world camera is exhilarating and a great way to bring the outside into the classroom. It's simple: take a picture, download the picture, print it out, and display it in the classroom.

The following are a few tips to consider before handing the camera over to young children:

- Make sure the camera is durable and can withstand some mishandling or possibly getting dropped. Children are active in nature so the camera may get jostled around a bit.
- Choose an inexpensive camera, but don't buy a kid's camera as they typically do not take quality photos.
- Give verbal warnings about the camera's fragility. Be close by to monitor the children's handling of the camera.
- Provide basic instructions about how to use the view finder, focus button, and keeping the camera steady while taking the picture.
- Encourage children to think of the smallest creatures and plant life such as butterflies, worms, wildflowers, and trees.
- Show children how to get close or zoom in on the subject if they want to see the details of their specimen.
- Once back in the classroom, give children an opportunity to view their images and make decisions about which pictures to print. Attach an activity to the image such as (1) finding out more about the photo's subject through the Internet; (2) sketching or sculpting the child's favorite subject; or (3) labeling the photo.

Although children enjoy being out in nature and love using the camera, be sure to teach respect for the outside world. Be careful not to trample plants and flowers or disturb critters in their homes. The best part of photographing the great outdoors is being able to further enjoy nature inside as well.

029
DISPLAYING NATURE COLLECTIONS

When we think of natural museums or art museums, our mind often conjures up large buildings with floors and floors of artifacts and displays. However, young children don't need grandeur or large spaces to understand the importance of their found nature collections. Even the most common and overlooked bits of nature can become objects of fascination if given the opportunity to be front and center in the classroom. The following are several ideas to incorporate children's found nature collections into your classroom:

CLASSROOM NATURAL MUSEUMS
Find a display case, table, or shelving unit that becomes the children's special space for found objects and position it in a prominent area in the classroom. Offer interesting see-through jars and low-sided containers for children to use when displaying their found items. Provide display stands and pedestals for children to use. Include 3 by 5-inch index cards for children to make identification tags.

Whenever going outside, bring along a unique collecting basket for children to gather their treasures. Before coming inside, have the children determine what items will be displayed in their nature museum. Elect a naturalist to keep the museum neat and tidy as well as a curator who is responsible for displaying the children's wonderful found treasures. Encourage children to frequently change the museum displays to keep interest anew.

CORNER TREE
A few pieces of plywood, wood stain, and some cement screws makes for an easy, affordable tree designed to highlight children's projects.

NATURE CHAIR
Be on the lookout for an interesting chair that you could use for displaying children's special objects found while outside, at the park, or on a nature hike. Interesting chairs can be found most anywhere—garage sale, recycle shop, or resale store. You might even find a unique chair in your basement or grandmother's attic. The special chair can either be placed outside the classroom door or inside the classroom. Chairs made from natural wood with hard, flat seats and spindled backs work best if the chair will be inside. Select a chair made of durable material if it will remain outside.

Whenever outside, encourage children to look for special nature treasures. On hikes, bring along a handled bucket for their collections. A bucket with handles makes it easier to carry along while on a hike. Elect a child responsible for carrying the bucket and keeping prized finds safe and sound. Or, place a large basket or bin on the playground so children can easily store their found objects. Once inside, give children the opportunity to determine which treasures they will display and how they will look.

Provide 3 by 5-inch cards and markers or pencils for children to create identification cards for their found objects and to autograph their finds. Children can also write where they found the natural object and the date of discovery.

FLOATING NATURE BOWL
The natural world is thick with possibilities for discovering and collecting. Invite children to display their natural collections by beautifully floating them on water in a container or unique bowl.

BEAUTY AT THE SNACK TABLE
Natural elements infuse beauty into the classroom. Oftentimes, we think that bringing nature to the classroom needs to be complicated, time consuming, and expensive, but it doesn't have to be! A simple sandwich bag folded down with a child-found pinecone and tree cookie brings lovely elegance to the middle of the lunch table.

Nature is a tool to get children to experience not just the wider world, but themselves.
Stephen Moss

PART TWO
Creating

CREATING

Find nature in unexpected places. Look . . . and you will see. Wherever you are and whenever it may be, look . . . and you will see. Whatever you are doing, no matter how mundane or insignificant to you, look . . . and you will see. Take a moment right now to look . . . and you will see.

Put down this book and look outside the window, stand at your opened front door, walk outside, stroll along the neighborhood sidewalk, or walk on a woodland path . . . and look for nature.

When you begin to open your eyes and purposefully notice, you will find nature all around you: malls, schoolyards, neighborhood yards, parking lots, railroad stops, subway platforms, roadsides and lakesides, sidewalks, golf courses, alleyways, cemeteries, airports, and parks. Now that you have found nature, what are you going to do with it?

One idea is for children to create art. It is important to understand that creating art with nature is distinctively different from the traditional classroom arts and crafts project. Art is an expression of children's thoughts, emotions, and their understandings of the way the world works. With nature art, children use the elements of the Earth to tell their stories—it is about the process and the journey of creating with nature so that the children's artwork can never be replicated.

Conversely, traditional classroom arts and crafts projects are more interested in a tangible output or replicated end product, which in most instances, means every child's work looks pretty much the same as everyone else's. It's about googly eyes, cotton balls, pipe cleaners, and pieces of precut construction paper.

Let's do away with arts and crafts projects, and in their place, offer opportunities for children to express their emotions through creating with nature. The experiences and ideas included in this section, *Creating*, will help children begin to understand the beauty of nature and become familiar with its textures, patterns, and colors—making magnificent nature the children's art subject.

Art comes from the child's heart.

Arts and crafts come from the teacher's mind.

Gyotaku is a wonderful project for young children because it combines many different types of learning experiences.

CREATING

030
JAPANESE GYOTAKU (FISH PAINTING)

Gyotaku is a Japanese word that literally means *fish impression*. Over 100 years ago, Japanese fishermen used Gyotaku or fish imprints as a way of keeping record of their daily catch. Fisherman would apply a black ink—or Sumi ink made out of vegetable oil soot—to one side of their catch, press rice paper on the inked fish, and then rub the paper to make an exact replica of the fish. Although Gyotaku was originally used to document the fishermen's catches, fish printing has evolved into a traditional and highly prized art form in Japanese culture.

Gyotaku—in its truest form with a real fish—is a highly sensorial learning opportunity. Painting a fish is fascinating, weird, smelly, and pure fun for young children. If, however, you are not the adventurous type and do not want to work with real fish, rubber fish can be purchased for practicing the art of Gyotaku.

Here are step-by-step directions on how to create beautiful fish prints by practicing the traditional art of Gyotaku with young children:

1. Procure a good-sized and large-scaled fish. Purchase from the grocery store or fish market, go fishing and catch one, or use a fish replica.

2. If using a real fish, prepare the fish before doing the project. Preparation includes washing the fish with water and a sponge to remove mucous and debris. While rinsing the fish, take extra care with the gill area because this is a spot where fish fluids often hide. Adding table salt or lemon juice helps to remove slime from the fish's body. Dry the fish using paper towels being sure to pull open the fins and dry repeatedly. If children assist in cleaning the fish, provide thick rubber gloves to prevent poked fingers from the fish's fins or gills. Everyone's hands should be washed after handling the real fish.

3. Place the fish on a tray covered with wax-paper, a piece of cardboard, large rag, or tinfoil. A top from a cardboard box (i.e., copy paper box cover) also works great because its high sides catch stray paint, and it can be thrown away when the project is finished.

   NOTE: This project is messy so covering the entire table surface with newspapers, sheets, or old tablecloths is a wise precaution. Remember, art projects do not always need to be done on a table. Place a tarp on the tile floor and you have a huge place for children to paint fish.

4. Place some water-soluble paint or printing ink into small trays. Washed Styrofoam™ vegetable trays from the grocery store work perfectly for this project because the sides of the trays help capture excess paint. Since the trays are disposable, they also make for quick and easy cleanup.

5. Ink up a brayer (hand roller) or small paintbrush and apply the paint evenly on the fish with a thin layer of water soluble paint or ink. Many types of paint work beautifully for this project including tempera paint, India ink, Speedball printing ink, non-toxic Sumi ink, poster paint, and acrylic paint.

HINTS:
- If you use Sumi ink, be very careful because the ink is permanent. You also might want to have children wear rubber gloves. Water-based paints are best to use with young children.

- Blotting the fish with a cotton rag immediately after painting and before the next step helps create a higher-quality imprint. If you have too much paint, the imprint becomes smeared; and too little paint doesn't allow for a good transfer of the fish's image.

CREATING

FISH PAINTING PROMOTES YOUNG CHILDREN'S LEARNING!

SCIENCE	WRITING	LANGUAGE
- Fish Diversity	- Creative Writing	- Enriched Vocabulary
- Fish External Anatomy	- Species Identification Cards	- Gills, Fins, Lateral Line

MATH	ENVIRONMENTAL EDUCATION	ARTISTIC EXPRESSION
- Measuring Parts of Fish	- Food Chain	- Experience Rich Colors
- Counting Fins & Scales	- Clean Waters	- Add Environmental Details

ART MEDIUMS	READING	ART TOOLS
- Relief Painting	- Fiction Books about Fish	- Brayer
- Imprint & Block Art	- Non-Fiction Books on Fish	- Paint Brush

- If you are using a real fish, wipe off its eye with a Q-tip after applying paint and before proceeding to the next step.

- Typically, Gyotaku fish imprints use black ink, but it is also fun to experiment with different colors.

6. Place a thin-type paper on top of the fish. Beginning in the center, press the paper down on the fish and rub gently, making sure to slide your hand or fingertips over the entire fish and hold the paper steady. Try to keep creases out of the paper. This step works best if there are two people involved: one for holding the fish and one for working with the paper. Once the paper has been firmly pressed on the fish, gently peel off the paper to reveal a gorgeous imprint!

HINTS:

- If using a real fish, place foam material under its head and tail to support these areas when painting.

- To get a better imprint of the fish's fins and add beauty to the imprint, place the fish on a foam board and then spread out the fins. Use straight pins to position the fish and pin open the fins. This job is best done by an adult and only if there are enough adult eyes to supervise.

- Thin (but strong) paper works the best for fish printing including silk, rice, copy, Manila, Shoji, Kozo, and high-quality construction paper that is thinly cut. Whichever paper you decide to use, make sure it is large enough to cover the whole fish, thin enough to easily drape into the fish's contours, but thick enough so it won't tear.

7. Place the print in a safe spot to dry. Once dry, children can paint the fish's eye and add color to the fins or gills if desired. Frame the fish imprints.

CREATING

Additional Hints for Gyotaku:

- Gyotaku fish painting is stunning. Provide pieces of paper to children that will fit into standard-sized picture frames because it's highly likely these imprints will be transformed into beautiful displays for the classroom wall or perhaps in the science area.

- Gyotaku takes time, patience, and practice. Give children plenty of opportunities to paint the fish over and over again in order to perfect the art.

- Fabric (especially cotton or muslin) can be used in place of paper. Be sure to use paint especially designed for fabric.

- Once a child has finished an imprint, it is time to wash off the fish and begin anew. Remember to pat the fish dry after cleaning off the paint.

Working with rubber fish for Gyotaku has several advantages:

- Real fish tend to be slippery, whereas rubber fish don't move around because the back of the replica is flat.

- Rubber fish can be used over and over again, while the real fish must be purchased every time, which is cost prohibitive. Also, finding whole fish still equipped with eyeballs and scales may be challenging, especially if you live in a rural community.

- Rubber fish do not smell.

- Real fish need to be prepared prior to the project.

- Rubber fish do not care what the temperature is, but real fish must be kept in a refrigerator or cooler to prevent spoilage.

Resource Guide

Over in the Ocean: In a Coral Reef by Marianne Berkes

Under the Sea by Christiane Gunzi

A Swim Through the Sea by Kristin Joy Pratt

Eyewitness: Fish by Steve Parker

Eyewitness: Pond and River by Steve Parker

What's It Like to Be a Fish? by Wendy Pfeffer

A Good Day's Fishing by James Prosek

About Fish: A Guide for Children by Cathryn Sill

Fabulous Fishes by Susan Stockdale

Fish Faces by Norbert Wu

H is for Hook: A Fishing Alphabet by Judy Young

Fish replicas (fresh and salt water) can be found online with several companies including **enasco.com**, **dickblick.com**, and **acornaturalists.com**. The rubber fish are realistic, life-sized replicas with a flat back for easy handling. Examples include bass, piranha, angelfish, trout, flounder, and bluegill.

CREATING

031
BRANCH WEAVING

Be on the lookout for a fairly good sized tree branch that is forked. The fork section of the branch is used for the weaving. After showing children the forked branch and explaining the weaving project, go on a nature hunt to find things that are long and pliable to weave such as grass, skinny twigs, leaves, flowers, bark, and pine needles. Wrap string, ribbon, or yarn in a figure-eight design around the forked area of the branch to create a loom. Let the children weave any of the items they have found in nature. This is a good trial and error experiment as there may be some found objects that are not soft and pliable enough to be woven through the branch loom.

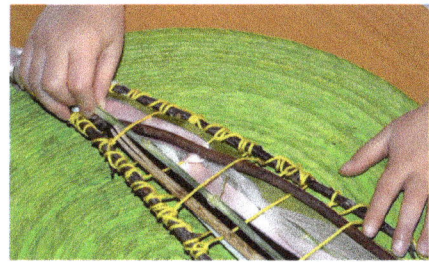

032
TREE COOKIE WEAVING

A tree cookie also makes a terrific weaving base—simply screw eye hooks into the cookie and find natural materials to weave.

033
NATURE'S SPIRALS

Hand-printed natural objects are a direct impression of the outside world. Freshly picked or just found bits of nature, which are carefully painted and pressed to paper, fabric, tiles, or other surfaces transform these objects into beautiful reflections of the natural world in which we live. The forms, textures, and most importantly, the patterns of nature are undeniably fascinating and orderly to adults. However, enjoying the beauty of nature's patterns is not just limited to adults as children are equally fascinated by nature's intricacies.

The patterns of nature are right before our eyes. Just stop and take a minute to discover the beauty of the lines on a freshly mowed lawn, the rows of corn stalks shifting back and forth in the gentle summer wind, or the crystal frost on a wintery frozen window pane. Encourage children to search for these intriguing patterns in nature by looking for basic shapes (i.e., circles, ovals). Try photographing (and printing) the patterns. Experiment with texture rubbings so children can see and touch nature's patterns. Encourage children to compare and describe the patterns; sketch the patterns with colored pencils or watercolors; and replicate the patterns with various art techniques such as paper rolling, clay modeling, or fabric weaving.

Spiral patterns especially hold a certain fascination for adults and children. Spirals are outwardly complex, yet simple and intriguing, and they abound in nature. Just take a careful look around and count how many spiral patterns you can find in seashells, plants, flowers, animals, and even the Earth and galaxies around us. This beautiful paper basket is a nod to nature's spirals. It was made by children by tightly rolling individual paper strips into spirals and gluing them together to form a colorful (and quite sturdy) bowl.

Follow these steps to create your own spiral paper basket:

1. Cut construction paper into ½ by 6-inch strips using a variety of colors and paper textures.

2. Demonstrate to children how to form the spirals by wrapping each paper strip around a pencil, and then carefully remove the pencil from the center of the rolled strips. Pinch your forefinger and thumb in the middle of the coil and gently pull. Put a dab of liquid glue under the tail end of the paper strip and press to the coil. Hold until dry. Repeat this process until there are about 350 spirals.

3. Cut out a 3-inch diameter cardboard circle. Glue the coils face down on the circle leaving no spot vacant. Once dry, begin building the sides of the basket by standing the coils on end and gluing to the cardboard base and on the side of the coils on the bottom. Continue gluing the spirals around the cardboard base and work your way up. To create a bowl-shaped spiral structure, put fewer and fewer spirals as you build up.

Resource Guide

Swirl by Swirl: Spirals in Nature by Joyce Sidman celebrates the beauty and value of spirals in nature. Fiddleheads, elephant tusks, crashing waves, and spiral galaxies, this book not only celebrates the beauty, but the usefulness of this fascinating shape.

If we pay attention, nature has the profound power to awaken the place of beauty within us. We have the capability to recognize the beauty and mystery of nature because that beauty and mystery are at the heart of our being. It is in all the life around us—it is us.

**Laura Bethmann
from *Hand Printing
from Nature***

CREATING

034
WOODBLOCK ARTISTRY

The face of a tree stump reveals its unique history through its shape, pattern, color, and various irregularities. These interesting characteristics can be transferred from stump to paper in wondrous detail—capturing every ring, line, mark, and crack. Woodblock or relief prints are easy for children to do.

Follow these steps:

1. Find dead or damaged logs in the forest, nearby nursery, or local farm. A tree stump, thick slice of a branch, or large tree cookie works great for woodblock prints.

2. Prior to bringing the wood piece into the classroom, brush off debris. You can even scrub with soap, a wire or steel brush, and water.

3. If you are concerned about splinters, smooth out the wood's surface with a hand planer, palm sander, or electric belt sander. The goal is to sand the woodblock as smooth as possible so that the paper will not wrinkle when it is placed on the wood.

4. Roll black tempera paint on the wood's surface. Experiment with the thickness of the paint to see what works best for the relief prints. Children might want to experiment with the effects of different colors on the woodblock relief print. Dark colors might work better—or maybe not.

5. Use thin paper, which allows children to see the print emerging on the backside of the paper. Taping the paper to the wood prior to rubbing helps reduce slippage. After the paper is placed on the wood, children can use their hands by carefully pressing or rubbing on the wood's rings. A brayer or wallpaper roller can also be used.

6. Lift the paper from the wood and place on a flat surface to dry. You can try several versions from the same paint run. Experiment by adding a contrasting color on the wood block or spray with water to create variations to the wood prints.

CREATING

035
TWIGGY TIC-TAC-TOE

Invite children to find small twigs that can be cut 3 to 4-inches long. Encourage children to tie the twigs together with string, yarn, or twist ties to form the "x." Use shells or flat stones about 3 to 4-inches in diameter for the "o" in the game.

Create a game grid by using permanent magic markers on a piece of burlap, poster board, or cardboard that is large enough to accommodate the game pieces. Or, make the game board from twigs.

036
TWIG EASEL

Display artwork with child-made easels made from sticks and thin wire. Sticks can also be held together with rubber bands, twist ties, or strong duct tape.

CREATING

037
STICKY STICKS

Sticks and clay are a great combination for creating sculptures. Simply use the clay for sticking the sticks together. The result? Sticky sticks!

CREATING

038
LEAF RELIEFS

Botanical relief printing is all about shapes, patterns, designs, and colors. When children hand-print a leaf, they see how the veins grow out from the main stem of the leaf and its basic form. Young artists see the repeated and regularly spaced patterns—branching, radiating, and spiraling. Hand-printed nature reliefs are direct impressions of nature. They are authentic and aesthetically pleasing to the touch, sight, and even smell with the leaves' earthy aroma.

Leaf reliefs can be accomplished with even the smallest of hands in a few easy steps:

1. Gather interesting leaves (or other natural objects) to print. The leaves from aspen or ginkgo trees are great for hand-printing. Although weeds aren't welcome in anyone's garden or yard, they make great objects for nature-printing. Queen Anne's lace is especially nice for hand-printing.

HINT: Encourage children to find optimum leaf specimens that are without nicks or rips, are fairly flat, and have a good painting surface.

CREATING

2. Place gathered leaves in plastic bags for transporting back to the classroom. Bring along sticky labels to document where you found the leaves and perhaps the leaf's identity (i.e., oak, maple). If the leaf was found under a tree canopy, take a picture of the tree for additional documentation.

3. Prep the leaves. Be sure the leaves do not have any moisture on them. Putting the leaves between pieces of paper towel and gently pressing down is an easy step children can accomplish. Also, press the found leaves in a book for about an hour to help smooth out the leaves' painting surface.

4. Get your ink or paint.

   HINT: The best ink for hand-printing is water-soluble printing inks or acrylic paint. For small leaves, use an ink pad. You can also paint leaves with dabbers or magic markers of different colors.

CREATING

5. For young painters, finding a surface for the leaf relief is easy and most can be found around the classroom.

   HINT: Newsprint, copier, or Manila paper provide inexpensive and receptive surfaces for hand-printing. Other interesting, but more challenging surfaces for hand-printing include plywood, drywall, fabric (i.e., muslin or cotton), and ceiling tiles.

6. The rest is simple. Paint the leaf with a very light coat of any type of ink or paint (i.e., acrylic paint, magic markers, dabbers, ink pad). Too much paint will result in the print smearing or not being able to see the veins or other features of the leaf. Cover the leaf with another piece of paper. Then carefully put the painted side of the leaf to the paper and encourage children to press gently with their fingertips, a brayer, or a rolling pin. Lift and voilà, a beautiful impression of nature.

Resource Guide

Trees, Leaves and Bark (Take-Along Guide) by Diane Burns

Tell Me, Tree: All About Trees for Kids by Gail Gibbons

The Tree Book for Kids and Their Grown-ups by Gina Ingoglia

beautyandwonderoftrees.org

039
PAINTED LEAVES

Leaves come in all different sizes, shapes and especially beautiful colors in autumn. Unfortunately, at the end of the fall season they lose their beautiful colors. Make the brown leaves look vibrant again by painting designs on them.

Follow these steps:

1. Place the leaves in a large hardcover book for several days to dry and flatten.

2. Although acrylic paint works best, using tempera paint mixed with a little liquid glue also makes the paint stick to the leaves.

3. Invite children to paint and watch the creativity happen!

GOOD LEAVES FOR YOUNG PAINTERS	
GINKGO	MAPLE
OAK	SYCAMORE
TULIP TREE	BEECH
ASPEN	COTTONWOOD
DOGWOOD	HAZEL

To draw you must close your eyes and sing.
Pablo Picasso

CREATING

040
PAINTED TREE BARK

Bark has such intriguing textures to explore—bumpy, smooth, prickly, and rough. Since no two pieces of bark are ever the same, opportunities for children's exploration are infinite. Including bark in the block area adds a whole new dimension to children's constructions—through children's imaginations, bark pieces are transformed into bridges, skyscrapers, and magical kingdoms. Putting bark in the science corner leads to investigations of its textures and ridges. Painting on bark creates an interesting and unique canvas.

If you live in a place where there are birch trees, birch bark is a good choice for children's paintings because it can easily be cut into appropriately-sized canvases. However, most types of tree bark will work for children's art. Foraging for bark is an easy and exciting task for children, but it is important to remember to only use bark from the branches or trunks of dead trees. Removing bark from live trees is harmful and should not be done. The best time for finding birch bark is in the spring or early summer.

HINT: To keep the bark from rolling up after you have collected it, lay flat, and put a heavy object on the bark to press it down. To make the birch bark more pliable and easier to use, soak in water for several days and then press it flat.

Delicious Bark Sandwich—Pretend, Of Course!

Make a buttery mixture of dirt, lake water, and pine needles. Heap this on a piece of birch bark and serve.

– From *Mud Pies and Other Recipes* by Marjorie Winslow

Painted Bark by Jeremiah, Age 3

This piece of bark (at left) was found by Jeremiah on a nature hike; he brought it into the classroom, painted it, and decided to put the painted bark back where he found it!

CREATING

041
DELICIOUS DIRT

Playing with dirt is deliciously fun for young children. Almost everyone knows the benefit of playing outside with dirt, but have you thought about the advantages of playing with delicious dirt in the classroom? Dirt tickles the hands and sparks young children's imaginations. Here are a few ideas to get you started:

DIRT CUPCAKES
In the home living area, invite children to create a thick mud mixture by mixing a small amount of water to dirt. Encourage children to use their hands to squeeze, squish, and play with the mixture until it is smooth. They can even try using some common kitchen tools such as a whisk, hand-crank mixer, or a potato masher. Next, drop the muddy mixture into cupcake liners that have been placed in muffin tins. Include small rocks, flowers, beads, and seashells for decorating the cupcake tops. Have a pretend bake sale for parents to see children's beautifully displayed baked goods.

CREATING

DIRT PAINTING

To make paint, mix dirt with water or a brown-colored tempera paint until the dirt is thin enough to use as paint. Provide paint brushes and pieces of cardboard canvases for the young Rembrandts in your classroom. Or, adding a small amount of dirt to finger paint creates an interesting texture for children to use. With your help, encourage children to do the mixing of dirt and paint.

DIRT DOUGH

Why does mud and dirt have to stay outside? Be brave and bring some mud and dirt into the classroom. Find some dirt on the playground, bring it inside, and make Dirt Dough.

042
SAND DESIGNS

Children naturally love to build, construct, and create. Encourage the architect in every child by offering interesting construction materials such as modeling sand, which is perfect for constructing.

Follow these steps:

1. Help children mix together 1 cup of sand, ½ cup of corn starch, and 1 teaspoon of alum.

2. Carefully add ¾ cup of very warm water and let the children stir vigorously. Add food coloring if desired.

3. Cook over medium heat until it is thick in the pan, and set aside to cool (adult job).

4. Once cooled, children can enjoy playing and manipulating the modeling sand and collaboratively creating houses, buildings, cities, and villages.

HINT: For long-time use, store the modeling sand in an air tight container or let dry in the sunshine for several days if you want the children's constructions to be more permanent.

As a child, one has that magical capacity to know a hundred different smells of mud.
Valerie Andrews

043
NATURE ARTISTRY

Andy Goldsworthy is a British artist and photographer known for his artistry in creating land (or ephemeral) art. Goldsworthy creates with materials he finds right beneath his feet or within an arm's length: twigs, stones, mud, berries, moss, ferns, leaves, pinecones, and acorns. With these easily accessible and found materials, he constructs visual beauty from natural objects (i.e., sculptures, mosaic-type patterns) on the ocean shoreline, the middle of a babbling stream, or by the side of a woodland path—existing for a moment in time until they are altered by animals, humans, or erased by the natural process. Simple and ordinary natural objects become extraordinary under Goldsworthy's enchanted touch and imagination. Give children inside opportunities to create land art just like Andy Goldsworthy. Simply find a small area in your classroom and declare it the Andy Goldsworthy studio.

Fill the studio with the following ideas that will transform an ordinary space into an extraordinary place for children to become nature artists:

- Check out Goldsworthy's photo-picture books from your local library and place them in the studio for children's inspiration. Encourage children to browse through the books' pictures checking out Goldsworthy's leaf and twig art as well as his rock sculptures.

- Go to the Internet and find images of Goldsworthy's art to download and post in the studio. Try framing some of Goldsworthy's work to hang on a wall or place on shelves.

- Depending on the size of the studio, set up several stations for children to work with different types of natural materials at each station. For example, you could fill a large wooden and edged tray with about 2-inches of sand collected from the nearby beach. Add sea pebbles, sea glass, coral, and various types of seashells. Or, fill a box lid or small drawer with dirt and provide various natural objects for children to arrange. Examples of natural materials include rocks, flat stones, flowers, moss, vines, lichen, pinecones, acorns, twigs, sea grass, buckeyes, grass, and leaves.

- Take pictures of the children's work, frame, and add to the Goldsworthy studio.

Resource Guide

All by Andy Goldsworthy:

Andy Goldsworthy: A Collaboration with Nature

Andy Goldsworthy: Rivers and Tides

Enclosure

Hand to Earth: Andy Goldsworthy Sculpture 1976-1990

Passage

Stone

Wood

CREATING

044
CREATING MANDALAS

Mandalas are circular designs that are thought to represent the universe's celestial circle of earth, sun, and moon. In addition to the religious, psychotherapy, self-reflection, and calming aspects of mandalas, they are also considered a traditional art form in many cultures. In the early childhood classroom, the meaning and constructing of mandalas could be more basic such as the circles representing children's immediate spheres of influence: friends, family, and community.

Help children understand the circular nature of a mandala by providing images, resource books, and an actual mandala. Solicit parents or friends to find an authentic mandala to bring into the classroom. Once children understand the basic concept of a mandala, it's time to get busy and create their own—or work with others to create a collaborative mandala. Assist children with making the mandala's base (i.e., circle drawn on a piece of plywood or cardboard; circle drawn in the sensory table's sand). Children can create circles within circles using a variety of natural loose parts such as rocks, stones, sea glass, seed pods, sticks, pinecones, glass beads, and wildflowers.

CREATING

045
MUSICAL MARACAS

Provide various seeds or beans for children to make shakers. You can use corn kernels, pinto beans, sunflower seeds, pumpkins seeds, watermelon seeds, or chia seeds. Small pebbles can also be used. The idea is to provide a variety of natural objects for the maracas so the sounds will be different. Collect plastic bottles with lids for the maracas' base. Encourage children to fill their bottle with a variety of natural items and to experiment with the sounds: loud, soft, soothing, and exciting. Close your eyes and listen carefully to the sound of the maracas. What natural item is inside?

Another type of maraca can be made with an oblong dried gourd. Encourage children to inspect the gourd to be sure it is free of any nicks or dents. Soak the dried gourd in a bowl of water for 24 hours. Punch out a small hole on one side of the gourd (adult job). Help children shake out the dried seeds and then place the gourd in a sunny spot in the classroom to completely dry. Once dry, invite children to place small pebbles in the gourd's hole and cover with masking tape. Paint the entire gourd with a mixture of tempera paint and liquid glue (about 50-50). The liquid glue will adhere to the masking tape and make the maraca bright and shiny. Then shake, shake, shake!

The soft pinging of seashells blowing in the wind is nature's music!

CREATING

046
STRINGING SEASHELLS

Stringing seashells is a wonderful way children can make a beautiful work of art. Regardless of whether they simply string seashells on a piece of twine, create a nature mobile, or construct a wind chime—the result is pure perfection.

Collect all sorts of different colors, sizes, and shapes of shells. Give a shout out to parents, friends, and relatives that you are collecting seashells for a class project. You may be surprised to discover that almost everyone has a few seashells hanging out around their house that they are willing to donate to a good cause.

The best kinds of seashells for stringing are those with natural holes, however, if you do need to make a hole in the seashell, follow these steps:

1. Use an electric drill with a 3/16-inch carbide drill bit (designed for drilling stone) to create the hole for stringing.

2. Anchor the shell in some clay to stabilize it and prevent it from cracking as you apply pressure to drill the hole.

Gather all sorts of items that could be used to string the seashells such as twine, thin wire, thread, yarn, and string. Also offer beads, straws, twigs, and other loose parts for children to use when creating their masterpieces.

CREATING

047
OK OKRA!

Although not a favorite vegetable for many, okra is an A-OK natural element to explore. If you have the outside space, growing okra is relatively simple to do. Just buy some seeds, plant according to the directions on the seed packet, water, and wait for the vines to appear. Okra prefers warm weather so wait until the ground has been warmed by the spring sun before planting—usually mid-spring is a good time to plant okra seeds or when the ground is 68°F. Okra plants prefer a home that has full sun. Also, they do not like water poured directly on them so watering around the plant is the best way to give the okra plant a drink of water.

Growing okra is perfect for young children because of its rapid growth. Many varieties of okra plants can grow 4 to 5 feet tall with some growing as high as 7 to 8 feet. Children will first notice a pinkish or yellowish bloom at the end of the plant's stalks. These beautiful flowers soon turn into edible okra pods. If you are growing the okra to eat, it is important to harvest the pods when they are tender and young. For recipe ideas on cooking okra, check out the Internet or a recipe book. Oftentimes, okra has a bad reputation for being slimy, but there are ways to eliminate this and make delicious and healthy dishes (especially soup, jambalaya, or stew).

In addition to being a tasty vegetable, use okra for other classroom experiences. Keeping okra on the vine and not picking it when young will cause the okra pods to become tough, woody, and inedible. Even so, they are a usable natural element when dried.

Follow these simple steps to dry the okra pods:

1. Cut the pod from the stem. Be sure to wear work gloves and wash your hands after picking as some varieties of okra can cause skin irritation.

2. Place the pods on a drying rack or paper towels and put the okra in a cool, dry place. It will take 2 to 3 weeks for the okra to dry completely.

3. When dried, the pods are pretty sturdy and hold up to children's handling.

Here are some ideas for using dried okra pods in the classroom:

- Dried okra pods are a great addition to the musical instruments area because the dried seeds inside the pod rattle when you shake it.

- Include the dried pods in the block corner to add to the excitement of children's constructions.

- Place dried okra in the home living center to add authenticity to children's cooking experiences.

- Dried okra makes a perfect addition to the science area as it is interesting to view through magnifying glasses.

- String dried okra into a nature mobile or paint and glitter the okra to make beautiful holiday ornaments.

CREATING

048
FUNNY NATURE FACES

Children enjoy handling authentic materials. Creating nature faces from gourds, pumpkins, and squash inspires children's creativity and satisfies their need to touch.

Using natural elements found in the forest (i.e., leaves, sticks, pinecones) is another idea for making funny faces. Either way, when finished, the nature items go back in the bowl waiting for the next Picasso's creation!

CREATING

049
PAINTING WITH KITCHEN SCRAPS

Nature provides so much variety that sometimes it is surprising what can be created from leftover kitchen scraps. The next time lunch is prepared for children, see what kitchen scraps can be salvaged in their next adventure with painting. Dip kitchen leftovers into paint and watch the excitement begin!

KITCHEN SCRAPS FOR PAINTING		
PEACH PITS	CARROT TOPS	CELERY STALK BOTTOMS
BANANA PEELS	AVOCADO SKIN & PITS	RADISH TOPS
TOMATO STEMS	POTATO PEELINGS	CITRUS FRUIT RINDS

> A child's attitude toward everything is an artist's attitude.
> **Willa Cather**

CREATING

050
BIRD WATCHING ART

In most parts of the world, birds are plentiful. For young children, birds are fascinating and beautiful creatures to observe as they flit from tree to tree in their fly-about neighborhood. Their songs and whistles capture children's attention and imagination. Why are the birds singing? What are they saying?

Enhance children's interest and learning about community birds by providing resources (i.e., books, images, videos) and experiences (i.e., constructing, painting, sculpting) to learn more about the birds in their area. Early spring is a great time to set up a bird watching station in your classroom. Locate the station near a window where children can easily see outside.

Provide bird watching resources such as binoculars, picture cards of local birds (easily found on the Internet), storybooks about birds, non-fictional resource books, and writing or sketching materials (i.e., clipboard, paper, colored pencils).

051
MILK JUG BIRD FEEDER

Neighborhood birds will flock to this recycled bird feeder made from an empty gallon milk jug.

Follow these steps—it's as simple as 1, 2, 3:

1. Cut 3 holes into the milk jug (adult job).
   - The first hole is for the bird feeder's door. Cut out a 3-inch circle a few inches up from the bottom of the milk jug.
   - The second hole is for the bird's perch. Punch a small hole right below the 3-inch circle. A large nail or hole punch works good.
   - The third hole is for the feeder's hanger. Poke a hole on both sides of the jug just below the jug's cap.

   Once the holes have been cut, thread a thin wire or thick twine through the holes and tie a double knot at the ends.

2. To decorate the feeder, invite children to gather leaves and small twigs. Glue the leaves on the jug's sides and the twigs on the jug's top for the roof. Be on the lookout for just the right sized twig for the bird perch. The twig needs to be just a little bigger than the hole so it can be wedged into the opening. Once the leaves and twigs are glued on and they have dried, paint over the entire milk jug with a layer of thinned-down Elmer's® glue.

3. Add birdseed and hang on a tree branch. Even though birds are small, they have big tummies, so be sure to check the bird feeder and refill when necessary.

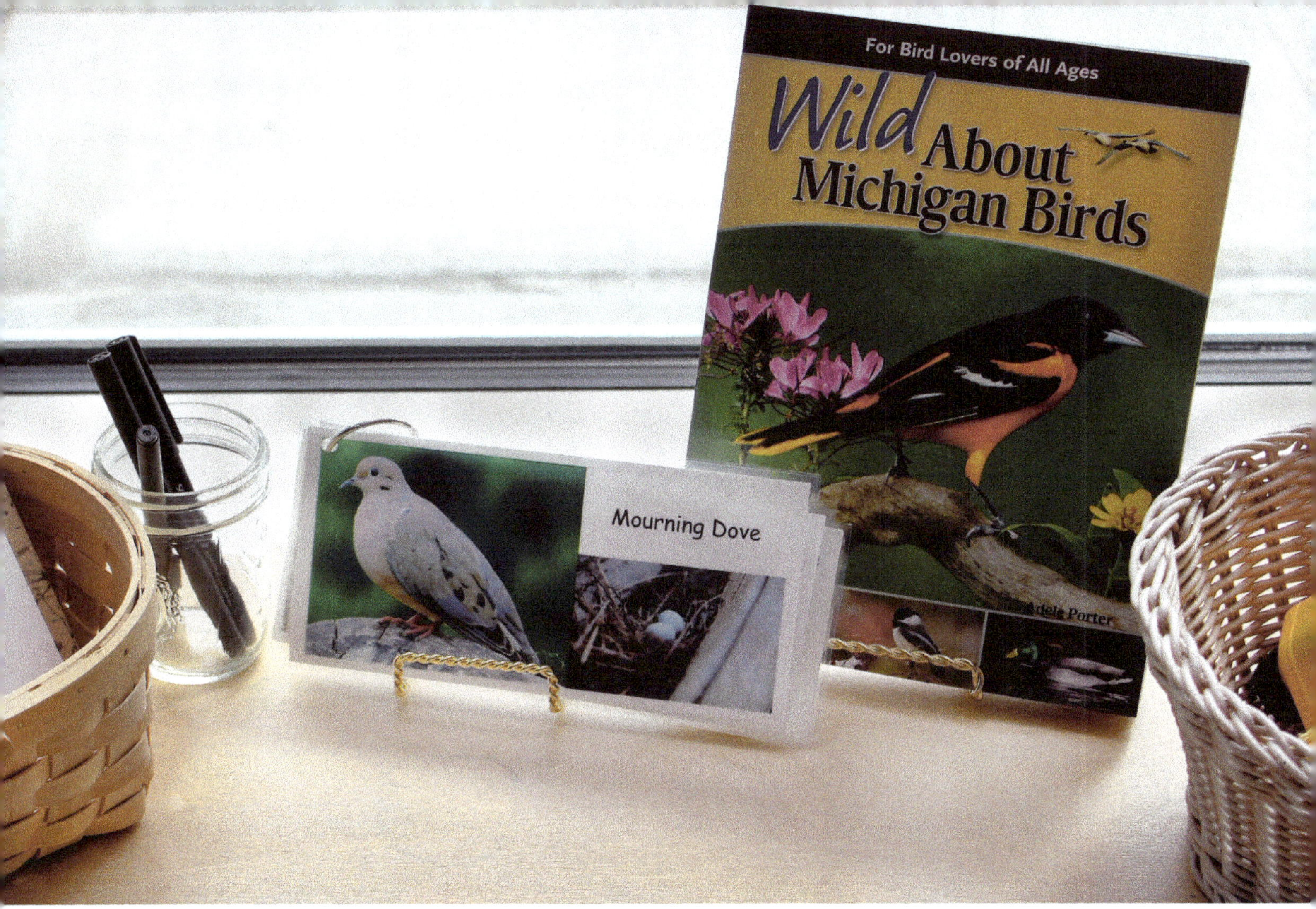
For Bird Lovers of All Ages
Wild About Michigan Birds
Adele Porter
Mourning Dove

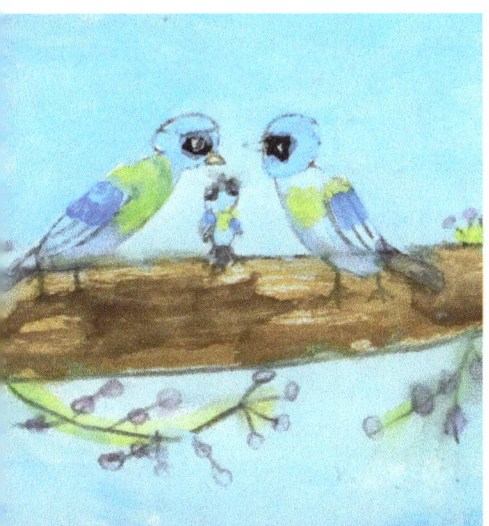

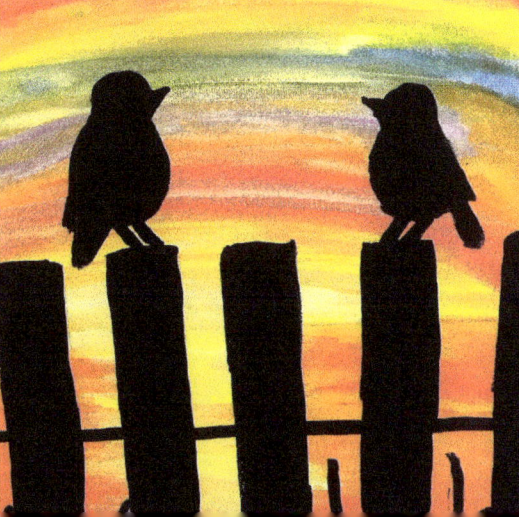

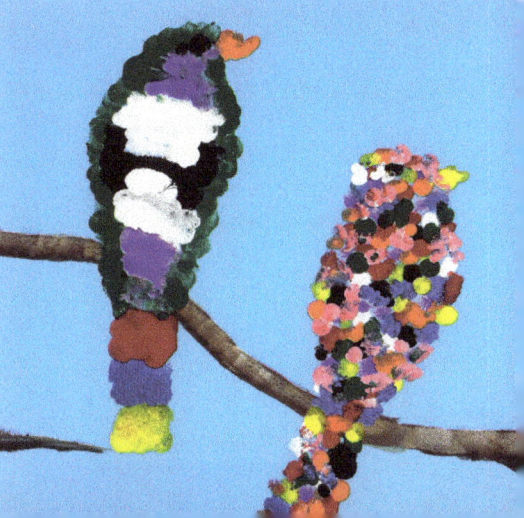

052
GOURD BIRDHOUSES

Autumn is a perfect time for finding gourds to be used for birdhouses. When selecting gourds from a garden, look for those whose stalks have turned brown or yellow. Using clippers, cut the gourds from their vine, leaving a few inches of vine attached to each gourd (adult job).

Once you have collected your gourds follow these steps to create birdhouses:

1. Prepare the gourds. Put the gourds in the sensory table filled with a mild solution of dish soap and water, and invite children to carefully wash. Place in a well-ventilated area and let dry for at least 48 hours. Once the gourds are completely dried, invite children to rough up the gourds' skins by lightly rubbing medium-coarse sandpaper over the outer surface. Be sure to exercise caution with the sandpaper so children do not bruise or sand through the outer edge of the gourd.

2. Cure the gourds. Return the prepared gourds to the well-ventilated space and keep there until fully dried or cured. It is important to rotate the gourds every third day to prevent rotting. Rotating, checking, and documenting the rotation of gourds on a daily basis is a good responsibility for children. The drying time is dependent on the gourds' size and shape. Gourds with long, skinny stems have a tendency to dry out faster. The drying out process takes at least 2 weeks and sometimes longer (up to 4 weeks).

3. Make the birdhouse door. Once the gourds are completely dry, begin making the birdhouses by creating a hole for the bird to enter its new home. Use a doorknob hole cutter or a knife just like you would for a jack-o-lantern to make a 2-inch opening in the gourd, and also to loosen up the seeds and gourd's interior pulp (adult job). When cutting the hole, place the gourd on a table so it doesn't roll around. Drilling or cutting the birdhouse door is easier than you might think because gourds usually have the consistency of thin plasterboard. After the doorway is cut out and the gourd's interior is loosened up a bit, invite children to scoop out the gourds' seeds and pulp. Gooey tactile fun!

4. Seal the gourds. Prior to painting the gourds, it is best if you seal them with Thompson's® WaterSeal® to keep the gourds from getting mildew or rotting (adult job). You can do this by brushing on the sealer with a paint brush. After sealing, arrange the gourds on a tray or drying rack and place in a cool, dry space in the classroom (out of the way of children) allowing them to dry out. Do not put the gourds in direct sunlight.

5. Paint the gourds. Use exterior latex paint to cover the entire gourd (adult job). A white or other light-colored paint is best to keep the birdhouse cool in the summer. After the latex paint is dry, invite children to design and paint the birdhouses with a mixture of 75% tempera and 25% liquid glue (i.e., Elmer's® Glue). Once the paint is dry, spray with clear polyurethane or clear acrylic paint on the inside and outside of the birdhouse (adult job). Let dry for at least 72 hours.

6. Hang the gourd birdhouses. Using a drill with a ¼-inch drill bit, drill a few holes in the bottom of the gourd for drainage and two additional holes on the top of the gourd for wire or leather lacing in order to hang the birdhouses (adult job). Thread leather lacing or thin wire through the top two holes to make a loop for hanging the birdhouse. Find the perfect tree branch and hang for both birds and bird watchers to enjoy.

CREATING

GOURDS & SQUASH		
BUTTERNUT	BUSHEL BASKET	ZUCCA
LUMP-IN-NECK	CHINESE BOTTLE	SHORT-HANDLED DIPPER
KETTLE	POWDERHORN	BASKETBALL

What's the difference? A gourd is a hard-shell fruit that comes in many varieties of sizes, shapes, and skin surfaces. While some are good to eat, most gourds are usually dried and used as decoration (especially near the autumn holidays).

A squash is a type of gourd, but has a softer skin surface or shell (i.e., butternut) and is a source of food. Gourds make better birdhouses because of their hard surfaces, but squash are easier to cut the hole for the birdhouse door.

053
BIRD NESTS

To sanitize an authentic bird's nest, wrap in foil and bake at a very low temperature for 15 minutes.

◦ RECIPE ◦
Whoooo's Hungry?

All the little owls in your classroom will enjoy making this snack and then have a great time gobbling them up.

Here's what you need for each owl:

☐ 1 piece of toast (owl's face)
☐ 2 tablespoons peanut butter (owl's face)
☐ 4 banana slices (owl's eyes and ears)
☐ 2 blueberries (owl's eyes)
☐ 3 almonds (owl's beak and feet)

Invite children to spread the peanut butter on the toast and then decorate to represent an owl's face.

CREATING

054
PAPIER MACHE

In French, "papier mache" means chewed paper. Bring this long-lost art into your classroom by turning wet and wrinkled paper into works of art. One simple idea for papier mache is to apply wet or chewed paper to a blown-up balloon, small bowl, or other similar container to make the object's simple shape. A round balloon, for example, makes a perfect octopus head or a fish's body. Or, a margarine container is a great base for a turtle's body.

To make papier mache, mix 2 cups of water and 1 cup of flour in a bowl to create a thin paste mixture. Let the children mix with a whisk until smooth. Use this paste to make the chewed paper for the papier mache. Cut 1-inch by 6-inch strips of paper (newspaper works best) and dip into the paste mixture. Pull the strips of paper out of the paste mixture and wipe off any excess. Apply to the balloon or container until the base is completely covered. Let the papier mache dry overnight or for longer if needed. Break the balloon or carefully pull the container from the papier mache. Decorate the object with acrylic paint and other loose parts such as sea glass, small pebbles, or seashells.

055
CEILING TILE FLOWER

Many buildings and rooms have drop ceilings, which at times can leak, resulting in the need to change an old piece of ceiling tile for a new one. Use the old ceiling tiles for artwork canvases. Use different colored duct tape for a colorful frame-like border.

CREATING

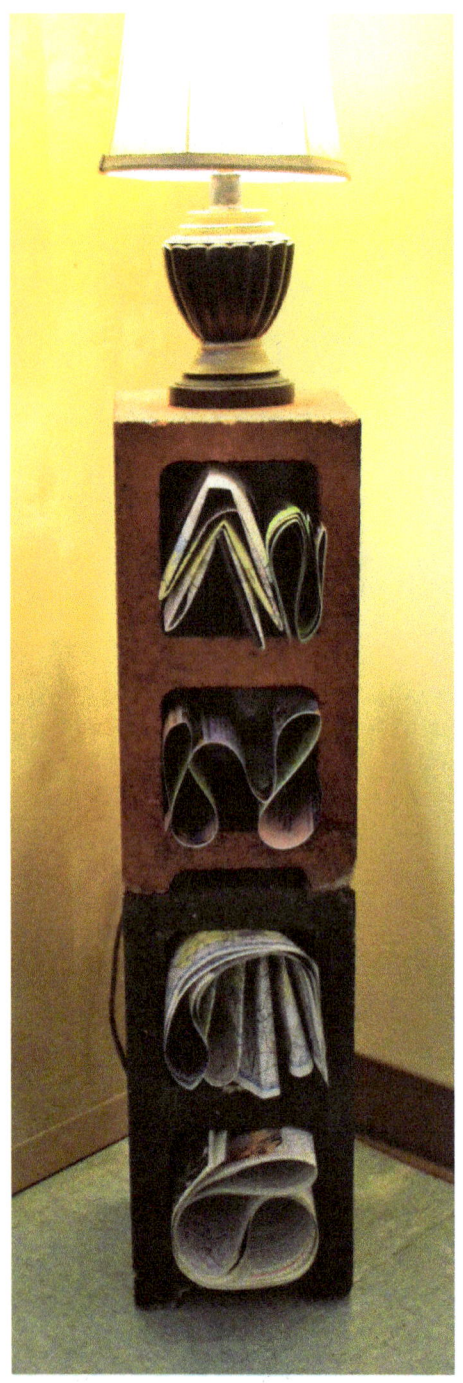

056
PRETTY BRICKS

Collect cinderblocks or bricks from a home improvement store or discards from a neighborhood construction site. They can be used for storing learning materials, as a classroom décor element, and as an added play component in the block center. Painting the blocks in a variety of colors gives children connection to classroom furnishings and a unique expression of their creativity.

CREATING

057
WILDFLOWER POUNDING

By definition, wildflowers are not intentionally planted or seeded by humans, but grow freely without human intervention. They grow in the wild—next to sidewalks, in vacant lots, and beside roads. Wildflowers are abundant and stunningly beautiful: bluebonnets, wild bells, blue buttercups, daisies, cornflowers, pink blankets, Queen Anne's lace, and violets.

Wildflower pounding is hammering a flower until you have art. Just imagine this idea: children making gorgeous works of art with no paint! Who would think that something as simple as wildflowers (or even leaves from a houseplant) and a wooden mallet or rubber-tipped hammer could produce such beautiful and inspiring images? Transferring the wildflower's pigment directly from a flower or leaf onto fabric is remarkably simple.

Follow these steps to create exquisite botanical impressions:

1. Prepare the fabric. Muslin is recommended, but any lightweight, plain fabric can be used as long as it is 100% cotton. Prior to using, wash the fabric (in a bucket or washing machine). Adding 3 tablespoons of washing soda to every gallon of water and rinsing several times will remove the fabric's sizing, which will make the flower pigment a more brilliant color.

    HINT: The most popular brand of washing soda is Arm & Hammer,™ which comes in a yellow box and can be found in the laundry section of the grocery store (don't confuse baking soda with washing soda, baking soda also comes in a yellow box, but is usually located in the baking section of the store).

2. Rinse the fabric several times to be sure that the washing soda comes out. Then, put the fabric in a bucket filled with hot water and 8 tablespoons of alum. Leave the fabric in this mixture for at least 8 hours or overnight. Take the fabric out of the water (do not rinse), wring out, and spread on a table or outside sidewalk. Iron the fabric (adult job) and cut into desired-sized pieces.

3. Find a pounding board. A piece of plywood or cutting board works great. If you do not want the pigment from the flowers to stain the pounding board, tape a sheet of wax paper to it. Place a piece of the prepared fabric on top of the wax paper and tape to the board to keep it from slipping.

4. Gather wildflowers. Although any size, shape, or color work great, flat flowers with vibrant colors produce the best transfer of pigment to the cloth. Puffier flowers have more pigment juice making the transfer image blurry and not as clear as a flat, thin-type flower. Spring or early summer is a great time to find wildflowers. If there are no wildflowers growing nearby the classroom for children to collect, encourage families to join the wildflower search in their neighborhoods.

5. Invite children to place the flowers face down on the fabric in any pattern or design they wish.

    HINT: Place the flowers in a single layer with no overlapping for best transfer of the wildflower's pigment onto the cloth.

6. Challenge children to completely cover each flower with clear tape. Wide packaging tape works best.

7. Pound the flowers with a wooden mallet or rubber-tipped hammer for several minutes (in place of a hammer, use a large flat rock). Advise children to hold the hammer with both hands (to keep their fingers away from the hammerhead) and to pound evenly. When done hammering, peel back the tape and remove any flower residue.

8. Heat-set the flower pigment by placing a sheet of paper over the design and quickly ironing over the paper (adult job).

CREATING

058
POTPOURRI

Scout your local neighborhood for wildflowers. You may find flowers growing in a vacant lot, next to a sidewalk, or in a nearby park (be sure to ask permission when gathering flowers in a public area). If you are unable to locate wildflowers growing outside, perhaps you can make friends with a neighborhood florist to see if they would be willing to put aside and save brown-edged or slightly wilted flowers. Another idea is to ask parents to contribute their backyard garden flowers to the potpourri project.

Once enough flowers have been collected, engage children in carefully pulling off the petals. Dry the petals on a flat surface for 5 or more days. When the petals are completely dried, put in a large bowl, add scented oils with an eye dropper, and gently stir. Store the potpourri in glass, wooden, or ceramic containers in a cool place in the classroom. Have children carefully stir the potpourri once or twice a week. Add more scented oils to enhance the lovely smell of the dried flower mixture. Potpourri makes a wonderful handmade gift for children's families and friends.

POTPOURRI RECIPE
- ☐ 4 oz rosebuds
- ☐ 2 oz lavender flowers
- ☐ 1 oz marigold flowers
- ☐ 1 oz peony flowers
- ☐ 1 oz bay leaves
- ☐ 2 oz peppermint oil

CREATING

- ☐ 20 drops lavender oil
- ☐ 10 drops rose essential oil

NOTE: You really don't need a recipe for potpourri as most any type of dried flowers, herbs, or oils can be mixed together to create a wonderful, beautiful smelling mixture.

059
WILDFLOWER PERFUME

Saturate a sponge in mineral oil and place in a small jar. Fill the jar with freshly cut herbs or garden flowers. Place a piece of cheesecloth over the opening of the jar and secure with a rubber band. Next, place the jar upside down on a slightly larger jar and secure with tape. Replace the herbs or flowers each day for the next 3 days. Next, squeeze the sponge into a small jar, and inhale the beautiful aroma! Use the scented oil to make wildflower sachets or add to a basket of pinecones for a wonderful classroom aroma.

ೂ RECIPE ೲ
Pansy Pancakes

Pansies are the colorful flowers with the charming "faces" that children love. Because pansies are edible they can be added to salads, soups, and even pancakes.

Here is what you need for Pansy Pancakes:

- ☐ 1¼ cups flour
- ☐ 2½ teaspoons baking powder
- ☐ 1½ tablespoons sugar
- ☐ ½ teaspoon salt
- ☐ 1 egg
- ☐ 1¼ cups milk
- ☐ 3 tablespoons butter, melted
- ☐ Cinnamon shaker
- ☐ Butter and syrup
- ☐ Pansies (washed and drained on a paper towel)

1. In a medium-sized bowl, sift together flour, baking soda, sugar, and salt. In a separate smaller bowl, whisk together the egg, milk, and butter (children's job).

2. Slowly add the liquid mixture into the dry ingredients and stir until just mixed. Batter will be slightly lumpy (children's job).

3. Heat frying pan until hot and spoon 2 tablespoons of batter for each

pancake into the pan (adult job). Place a pansy in the middle of each pancake.

4. When bubbles appear on the pancakes, flip them over and brown on the opposite side (adult job).

5. Sprinkle the pancakes with cinnamon (children's job).

6. Put the pancakes in a warm oven or tent them in tinfoil until you have cooked enough for all the children (adult job).

7. Serve with syrup and butter (children's job).

NOTE: Making and eating pancakes outdoors is especially fun on a beautiful spring day. Use an electric frying pan to cook the pancakes!

Wildflowers can grow without any help from humans.
Sierra Elizabeth, Age 5

PART THREE
Thinking

THINKING

Children are born with an inherent enthusiasm for life. Listen to the fervor of a newborn's first loud cry, a toddler's jubilant laughter while being twirled around in mommy's arms, or preschoolers singing "Old MacDonald Had a Farm" at the top of their lungs. Witness the enthusiasm of an infant scooting across the floor to retrieve a rattle, a wobbly toddler taking their first steps, or a preschooler running with excitement and without abandon across the play yard. Yet, somewhere along the way, children's enthusiasm for life begins to fade or completely disappear.

Ask a group of 25 preschoolers if they are good at something, and they will all invariably raise their hands and enthusiastically proclaim their competency. Ask a group of 25 elementary students the same question and less than 50% will raise their hands, and only one hand will pop up when high school students are asked. So, what happened? More importantly, how can we help young children keep their inherent enthusiasm for life and learning?

Switch Gears

Our expectations for children's educational success is based on the achievement of basic academic skills (i.e., reading, writing, and mathematics). We foster this notion by stuffing children's minds—open your brain and let me stuff it with knowledge I think you should know. "This is red." "This is a square." "This is more and this is less." When we take on the role of a stuffer, there is an unfortunate tendency to resort to rote learning or memorization, and we fail to recognize that obtaining knowledge is not necessarily understanding.

Without understanding, true life-long learning cannot occur. It is time for early childhood practitioners to switch gears from a stuffer to a facilitator. It is time for us to stop dictating and controlling the process of learning. It is time to create enriched environments and to begin facilitating opportunities for young children's creative problem solving, discovery making, collaborating with others, and conducting enthusiastic investigations.

Enthusiastic Environments

Nothing dulls children's enthusiasm more than lack-luster environments filled with plastic and laminated cardboard, commercially purchased toys, and one-use learning materials. Instead, create enthusiastic environments where children can play without adult intervention; jump, sing, and dance; create and construct without any adult saying what to do and what not to do; be silly and fool around; have opportunities to make choices and decisions; and most importantly, have provocative, interesting, and engaging natural materials and objects to explore, investigate, and discover.

In this *Thinking* section, you will learn about ways to bring the wondrous outside world into your classroom and create exhilarating thinking and understanding experiences for young children to learn within the classroom's walls. The possibilities for nature-based enriched environments are endless. We must commit ourselves to create, encourage, and keep children's inherent enthusiasm for life and learning. We must begin, and we must begin now, with enthusiastic and powerful nature-based classrooms.

> *When you teach a child something, you take away forever his chance of discovering it for himself.*
> **Jean Piaget**

THINKING

060
NATURAL LOOSE PARTS

Over the past several years, the theory of loose parts has gained momentum and popularity in the early childhood classroom. In the 1970's, architect Simon Nicholson proposed the theory of loose parts. He believed that the presence of loose parts in our environment enhances and empowers our creativity. Nicholson defined loose parts as objects and materials that can be carried, moved, redefined, taken apart, redesigned, and put back together again—in infinite and creative ways.

The possibilities for loose parts from nature are truly endless. There are many reasons for including natural loose parts in the early childhood classroom. Because they are open-ended and have no specific purpose, loose parts from nature encourage creativity. They are sensory-based so loose parts promote active and hands-on learning. When children take apart, examine, and reassemble loose parts, they are practicing critical thinking skills and problem-solving skills. Finally, loose parts from nature are economically feasible. In fact, they are absolutely free!

> ### Resource Guide
>
> *Outside Your Window: A First Book of Nature* by Nicola Davies
>
> *Organic Crafts: 75 Earth-Friendly Art Activities* by Kimberly Monaghan
>
> *Nature in a Nutshell for Kids: Over 100 Activities You Can Do in Ten Minutes or Less* by Jean Potter
>
> *Nature Education With Young Children: Integrating Inquiry and Practice* edited by Daniel Meier and Stephanie Sisk-Hilton

THINKING

NATURAL LOOSE PARTS

PINECONES	IVY	SYCAMORE PODS	STUMPS
PEBBLES/STONES	RIVER ROCKS	WILLOW BRANCHES	CORN HUSKS
STICKS/TWIGS	PINE NEEDLES	ORCHID GRASS	PUMPKINS/GOURDS
SEASHELLS	TREE BOUGHS	VINES	COCONUTS
TREE BARK	TUMBLEWEED	CROSSWORT	DRIED OKRA PODS
BEACH SAND	LOGS/BRANCHES	ACORNS	FERNS
BUCKEYES	BEECH HUSKS	GRANITE ROCKS	BABY'S BREATH
FLOWERS	CATKINS	DRIFTWOOD	PUSSY WILLOW
DANDELIONS	PINE BRANCHES	GRASS CLIPPINGS	MOSS
GRAVEL	RUSHES	TREE COOKIES	ROSEMARY STICKS
SEEDS	PLUM TREE PINS	FRESH HERBS	LICHEN
TREE PODS	PLANTS	MUD/CLAY	QUEEN ANNE'S LACE
SEAGRASS	TREE BLOCKS	FIREWOOD	PITS
LEAVES	BAMBOO	SEA GLASS	FEATHERS

NOTE: *Nature is beautiful and welcoming, but she is also full of tricks and hazards. Beware of grass or ferns that cut, or berries and flowers that seem so attractive, but are highly poisonous such as mistletoe, honeysuckle, and snowberries.*

The creative mind plays with the objects it loves. Artists play with color and space. Musicians play with sound and silence. Children play with everything they can get their hands on.
Stephen Nachmanovitch

THINKING

061
SORTING BONANZA

Invite children to collect stones, twigs, leaves, and other natural materials of various sizes, colors, shapes, and textures. Encourage sorting, classifying, and categorizing by providing a container with plenty of unique spaces. Find resource books and place them near the collected materials to extend children's investigations.

Here are some ideas:

- A cardboard box that was once filled with crayons can hold natural loose parts instead.

- An assortment of baskets can be great for sorting experiences as well as provide a beautiful aesthetic.

- A wooden condiment tray is terrific for sorting, classifying, and categorizing.

- Utensil trays make great sorting containers, especially for small rocks.

062
ACORN ADVENTURE

In the autumn, go on a scouting expedition for acorns that have fallen to the ground from a mighty oak. To eliminate the possibility of small bugs emerging from the acorns, place the acorns in a low temperature oven (250°F) for approximately 15 minutes. Or, you can wash the acorns in warm, sudsy water. A little bleach also helps eliminate bugs.

Once disinfected, dry the acorns in a warm sunny spot for 72 hours. Then, remove the caps and invite children to paint the insides of the caps. Although acrylic paint works best, children can use tempera paint mixed with a small dab of Elmer's® glue. Children can enjoy a variety of thinking activities with the painted acorn caps:

MEMORY GAME
Best suited for two preschool players, the object of the game is to collect the most matching pairs. Lay 12 pairs of acorns, painted side down, on the table. The first player turns over a painted acorn cap and then turns over another cap. If the caps are the same color, the player keeps the two caps and is awarded another turn. The first player continues until they do not make a match. If there is no match, the first player returns the two caps to their original position. It is now the second player's turn. The game continues until all the acorns have been paired.

SORTING GAME
Best for one or two preschool players, the object of this game is to sort all the acorns by a specific characteristic such as size or color as quickly as you can. Lay all of the acorns on the floor. Use a timer or hourglass and see if the sorting of a certain characteristic can happen before time runs out.

THINKING

063

BALANCING NATURE

Take a nature walk to collect items such as shells, seeds, tree pods, stones, twigs, and leaves. Bring the found objects back into the classroom and use a balance scale to weigh each of the natural elements. Encourage children to determine how many small stones it takes to balance the weight of one large stone or how many small seashells it takes to balance the weight of a large shell. Or, invite children to predict which natural element weighs more or weighs less. Does the sea pod, for example, weigh more (or less) than the leaf? After children make their predictions, weigh the objects to see if their predictions were correct. The combinations are endless when you let children weigh and balance the natural items they have found.

THINKING

064
UNIT STICKS

Developed by Dr. Carolyn Pratt, unit blocks were designed to teach young children mathematical relationships and early math concepts. Unit blocks are very commonplace in early childhood classrooms and usually find a prominent place in the block center. The block area is a popular destination in the classroom, but often can be stagnant because few playthings are added to it throughout the year. Although a few traditional objects (i.e., vehicles, zoo or farm animals, road signs, or people) may be added to the block area, these items are typically plastic or commercially made.

Why not go against tradition and brighten up the block space by adding natural elements such as pebbles, tree cookies, or even tree twigs? You could, for example, replicate the unit block idea by creating unit sticks. Simply go outside and find some tree twigs that are all about the same size in diameter. A 2 to 3-inch diameter works perfect for unit sticks. Cut approximately 20 sticks each of the following lengths in inches: 12, 9, 6, 3, and 1.

Display unit sticks much the same way you would position unit blocks in the classroom. Or, put the unit sticks in a large wicker-type basket and place near the blocks. Arranging the sticks on top of the block shelf according to length (from shortest to longest) not only makes a beautiful display, it also offers children experiences in seriation. More importantly, you will find that adding unit sticks to the block corner increases children's creativity in block construction. The sticks may become a bridge for animals to cross over, a roof for a log cabin, or tree bases for the pretend playground. Because the sticks are open-ended and there is no preconceived notion of what they should be, the opportunities for children's constructions are limitless.

Use natural loose parts for mathematical experiences.

065
GEOMETREE!

Create geometric shapes out of twigs! Introduce basic shapes like the triangle, circle, square, and rectangle. All you need are sticks or twigs and something to hold them together as you put together the shape. You could use: twine, rubber bands, masking tape, bread twist ties, or floral tape.

Children could also make the twig shapes on a piece of paper and adhere with a little Elmer's® glue. Extend the experience by identifying geometric shapes in nature such as the spiral, hexagon, and star.

HINT: If you cannot find flexible twigs or sticks, try soaking in water for an hour and then gently bend around a plastic cup. Use a rubber band to secure in place and allow to dry overnight. There should now be a slight bend in the stick or twig to make circular shapes.

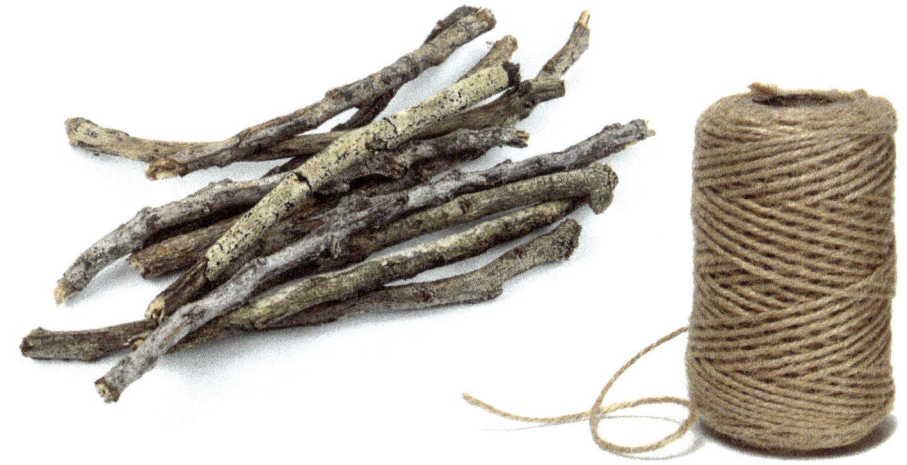

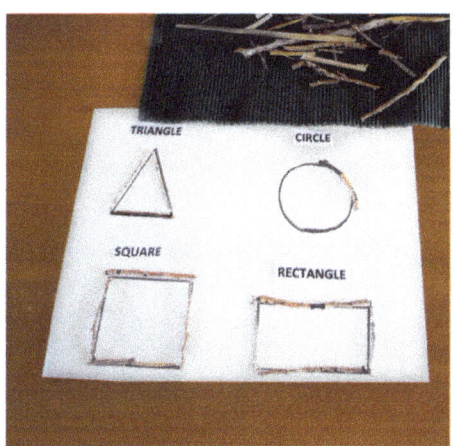

THINKING

066
ROCK COLLECTIONS

Rock collections (or any kind of collection) can help children begin to understand mathematical concepts such as seriation, categorization, and classification. Encourage children to collect as many different kinds of rocks from around the local community (i.e., playground, park, home) as they can. Find containers with numerous sections such as ice cube trays, muffin tins, or clean egg cartons and invite children to play. Rather than instructing them to perform a cognitive act (i.e., find all the small rocks), see where children's thinking and ideas lead them. Let the children decide what to do with the rocks and watch self-directed learning begin.

CHILDREN'S COLLECTIONS	
PINECONES	STONES
LEAVES	SEA GLASS
HEART ROCKS	GRASSES
INDIAN HEADS	FLOWERS
BUGS	BUTTERFLIES
SEASHELLS	FEATHERS
SEEDS	DRIFTWOOD
TREE PODS	FOSSILS
ACORNS	STICKS

067
RAINBOW ROCKS

All sorts of manipulative games can be done with rocks. For example, children can find, sort, and seriate rocks according to size. Make several sets of rocks distinguishable by color (i.e., red, blue, yellow). The object of the game is to stack the sets of rocks together by size and color.

> In matters of style, swim with the current; in matters of principle, stand like a rock.
> **Thomas Jefferson**

THINKING

068
STORY STONES

Children can share their own personal stories through story stones. Provide smooth, flat stones and permanent markers in a variety of colors, and invite children to draw images on the stones. For example, a sun might reflect a sunny day, a happy face might convey the feeling of joy, or a car might signify a vacation trip.

Resource Guide

The Real Story of Stone Soup by Ying Chang Compestine

Stone Soup by Ann McGovern

Rock Art!: Painting and Crafting With the Humble Pebble by Denise Scicluna

⁂ RECIPE ⁂
Stone Soup

Continue the Story Stone experience with the classic tale, *Stone Soup* by Anne McGovern, and make your very own magical soup with children, stone included!

You will need:

☐ 1 large smooth stone, scrubbed and boiled to sterilize
☐ 3 stalks celery, chopped
☐ 3 carrots, chopped
☐ 1 onion, chopped
☐ 5 small red potatoes, quartered
☐ 1 can diced tomatoes, drained
☐ ½ cup brown rice, cooked
☐ 5 cups vegetable broth
☐ ½ teaspoon dried thyme
☐ 1 bay leaf
☐ Salt and pepper, to taste

Read the story *Stone Soup* together. Put the clean stone in a large crock pot. Help children add all of the ingredients into the pot. Cover with the vegetable broth. Cook 2 to 3 hours on high, or until the vegetables are tender. Ladle the delicious soup into individual serving bowls and enjoy!

THINKING

069
I'M HERE TODAY!

There is nothing better than coming to school for the day because each day is an adventure! As a daily ritual, children begin the day by finding the rock with their name on it and placing it in the "Here Tray." Not only are they learning how to recognize their names, but children feel important and included in the classroom community.

> I am but a small child wandering upon the vast shores of knowledge, every now and then finding a small bright pebble to content myself with.
> **Plato**

THINKING

070
ALPHABET ROCK GAME

Use tempera paint (and then shellac over the paint) or fingernail polish (when children are not in the classroom) to write the letters of the alphabet on the rocks.

071
CAN YOU ESTIMATE?

Young children enjoy learning new words—the longer the better. The word "estimate" is a fun word to say and also a good mathematical word to know and understand. Rather than just guessing about something, invite children to estimate like scientists. One idea for exploring estimation in an authentic way is to fill a large jar with natural items such as pebbles, seashells, watermelon seeds, or small twigs. Encourage children to estimate how many items are in the jar. Have children write down their guesses on a pad of paper (along with their name) near the jar. After everyone has made their estimate, count the items in front of the children. The one with the closest guess is the best estimator! Some possible awards for the best estimator include: line leader, book holder, or maybe the best estimator gets to choose the next item to go in the jar.

NOTE: Parents might also enjoy being estimators and a part of the estimating fun!

THINKING

072
WRITING WITH NATURE

Young children and nature go together—just like peas and carrots. Likewise, young children and writing go together. Children enjoy expressing themselves by making marks such as dots, lines, and circles. Since this beginning form of writing is a precursor to literacy competency, it is important to foster this enjoyment by providing unique writing tools and surfaces and, more importantly, the freedom and luxury of time to explore these natural materials.

TOOLS	SURFACES	INKS
Nature provides all sorts of natural tools that can be used to write, draw, or paint.	*Writing on various surfaces results in different outcomes. Nature provides many textured surfaces—each one unique in their own way.*	*Nature offers a variety of elements that create different colors and are a natural ink or dye that can be used to add color to a variety of materials.*
STICKS/BAMBOO STICKS	BIRCH BARK	BERRY JUICE
ROCKS/STONES	TILE	MUD WATER
BOUND BUNCH OF GRASS	CORK	NATURAL DYES (see next page)
PINEAPPLE TOPS	SAND & MUD TRAYS	PENCIL
DANDELION HEADS	TREE STUMPS	CHARCOAL
BUNDLED PLANT CLIPPINGS	LIMESTONE & GRANITE PIECES	WATER COLORS
EVERGREEN BOUGHS	PARCHMENT PAPER	CITRUS WATER (orange, lemon, grapefruit, lime)
	PLYWOOD	
	WOOD VENEER	

THINKING

073
USING NATURAL DYES FOR INK

Use plant materials to make beautiful and soft ink colors. Experiment with various plant materials found while walking with children in the local community or nearby woods. Hard plants (i.e., sticks, bark, vine, roots) may need pounding to loosen their fibers, while softer plants (i.e., flower petals, grasses) can be used as is.

Follow these steps to make your own natural dyes for ink:

1. Wash plants (children's job).
2. Crush plant materials with rubber mallet or cut with children's scissors into medium-size pieces (children's job).
3. Put plant materials in a large pot, cover plants with cold water (just to the top of the plants), and soak overnight. Be careful not to add too much water (children's job).
4. Bring plant materials to a boil for 5 minutes, and then reduce heat to low. Gently simmer plant materials for approximately 1 hour or until water takes on the plants' natural color (adult job).

HINTS:
- A stainless steel pot works best, but is not necessary.
- Watch the water level to be sure that it covers the plant material; add more water if needed.

5. After cooling, strain the colored liquid from the plant materials (adult job).
6. Add 2 teaspoons salt and 2 teaspoons baking soda (children's job).
7. Enjoy writing with the natural dyes (children and adult's jobs).

Another way to use natural dyes in the classroom:
In addition to using the home-made natural dyes for writing projects, use the dyes for dying fabrics. Natural dyes are perfect for Tie-Dying T-shirts or a piece of cotton fabric for the home living area. Instead of using construction paper or purchasing brightly colored borders for the bulletin board, consider the idea of using natural dyes on cotton or muslin to use on the board's edges or background.

Remember, the natural dyes are soft colors so using white, off-white, or cream-colored fabrics work best. Place fabric in a warm dye bath solution for about an hour (or until liquid is completely cooled). Rinse the dyed materials several times in cold water and hang to dry. Water drips may stain the rug or carpet so be sure to either hang outside or over tile flooring.

THINKING

COLOR	PLANT MATERIAL
BLACK	Hickory or dogwood bark
BLUE	Alfalfa flowers/sunflower seeds
BROWN	Walnut shells/birchbark/coffee grounds
PINK	Red onion skins
GREEN	Moss/algae/leaves/spinach
PURPLE	Lilacs/blueberries/lavender
RED	Beets/cranberries/red raspberries
YELLOW	Yellow or white onion skins/carrots

Add food coloring, fabric paint, or acrylic paint to enhance desired color.

THINKING

074
NATURE READING NOOKS

Look around your classroom for a small empty space; you only need a couple of square feet. Define the space with a small braided rug and position a few cozy pillows for flopping on. Add a battery-powered lamp for ambiance, and if there is room, place a child-size rocking or beach chair to add to the comfy feel of the space.

Transform a refrigerator box into a terrific library filled with books. Let children decorate the outside of the box with tree sticks and small branches to represent a tree, forest, or woods. Cover the inside of the box by gluing real or construction paper leaves to it. Add some woodland-type pillows and a basket of books.

You're never too old, too wacky, too wild, to pick up a book and read to a child.
Dr. Seuss

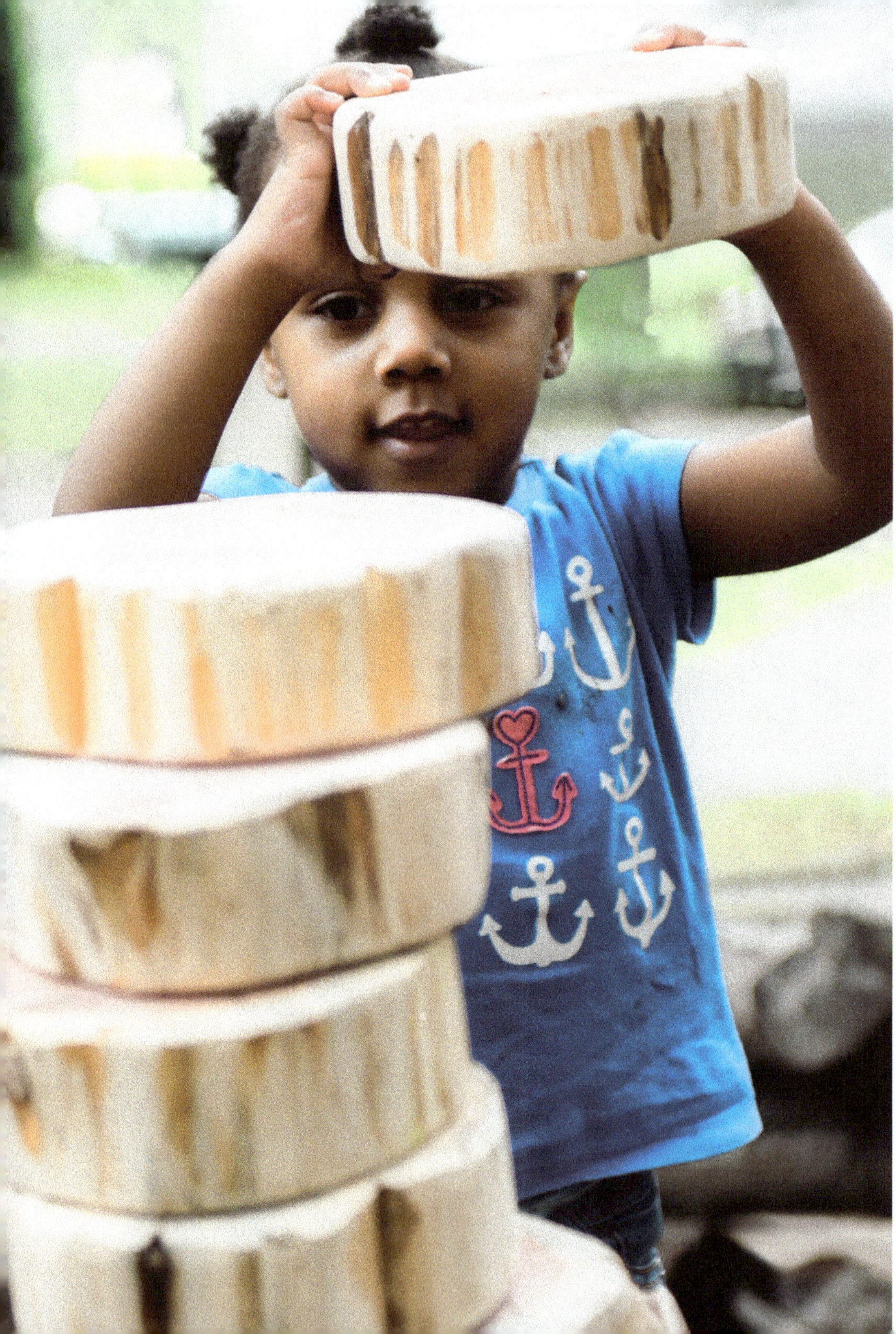

CHATILLON
How tall can you make your towe

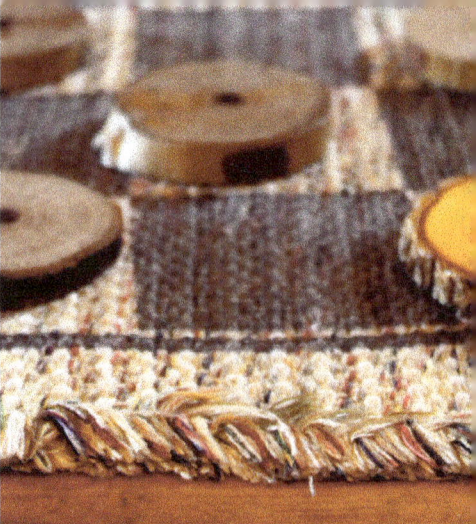

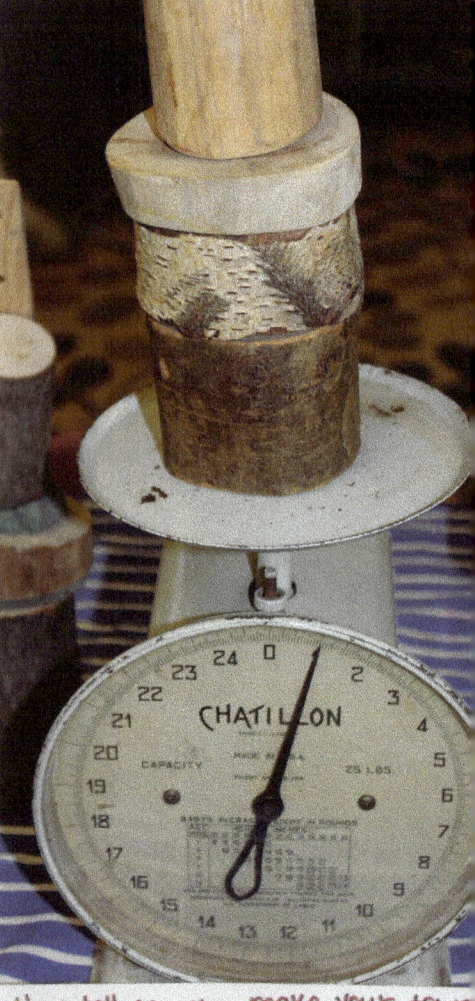

075
TREE COOKIE CONSTRUCTIONS

Tree cookies are beautiful pieces of nature made from tree branches that can be used in a variety of ways (i.e., games, construction, manipulation) to promote children's learning in the classroom. The best size of branch for a tree cookie is about 1-inch thick and about 3 to 6-inches in diameter, but the cookie's size will greatly depend on its use.

To get started making tree cookies, follow these steps:

1. Look for a tree branch. The best time to find a tree branch is after a windstorm when you can spot all sorts of branches in your backyard, neighborhood park, or roadside ditch. Keep your eyes peeled. You might be lucky and find someone clearing storm debris who is willing to slice up some freshly fallen branches, which are the best kind to use.

   NOTE: When looking for branches, be careful about tree service companies removing diseased trees. Although most branches are perfectly fine, some may be infested and unsuitable for use. Be sure to inspect the branch before putting it in your car trunk.

2. The most interesting tree cookies are made from tree species that have dark annual rings such as pine, spruce, fir, and walnut. Also, species such as spruce, fir, cedar, and pine are soft wood so they are easier to cut.

3. Use a large tooth pruning saw or electric saw to cut up the branch into tree cookies of the desired thickness (adult job).

4. Dry the tree cookies in the warm sun for a few days—don't forget to flip them over to dry the other side. The annual growth rings appear with drying.

5. Once the tree cookies are dried, children can enjoy sanding the rough edges with medium-weight sanding paper. Or, an adult can sand the cookies with an electric belt sander beginning with course and finishing with medium sandpaper.

6. If desired, coat the tree cookies with clear varnish or polyurethane to make them more durable (adult job).

THINKING

076
TREE COOKIE COUNTDOWN

Young children love to count everything—blocks, books, steps, people, and even their fingers and toes. All of this counting helps children learn important concepts like numbers, classification and categorization, quantities (i.e., more and less), and one-to-one correspondence. Capitalize on children's inherent desire to count by offering all sorts of natural objects perfect for counting such as pinecones, seashells, leaves, pods, seeds, and of course, the amazing tree cookie.

Follow these steps to make tree cookies for counting:

1. Cut a fallen branch into ½-inch circular pieces (adult job).

2. Offering small squares of sandpaper, invite children to smooth rough edges and uneven cuts.

THINKING

3. When the pieces are smooth and clean, mark each with a number 1 through 10 using a permanent marker.

4. Once the tree cookies are numbered, place in a basket along with other loose objects such as shells, rocks, and seed pods. Invite children to match the number on the tree cookie with the appropriate number of loose objects. For children's self-correcting, place the appropriate number of dots on the back of the tree cookie. For example, if the number on the front of the tree cookie is "5," you would make five dots on the back of it.

HINT: Children enjoy matching objects to the corresponding number by either stacking loose parts in front of, next to, above, or beneath the tree cookies so they are also learning position and spatial relationships in addition to numeral recognition and one-to-one correspondence.

077
TREE COOKIE ALPHABET & NUMERALS

Make your own alphabet and number charts from small tree cookies mounted on burlap or a bulletin board. Tree cookies are mounted to the base with double stick Velcro.®

In addition to math, use tree cookies for upper and lowercase alphabet association.

> *I cannot teach anybody anything. I can only make them think.*
> **Socrates**

THINKING

078
POUND AWAY

A tree cookie makes a great practice surface for learning how to pound and drive nails. Position a tree cookie (the thicker the better) in a safe and visible place in the classroom—a place where you can readily observe the children's pounding. For additional safety, limit the pounding to one child at a time. Be sure to provide safety goggles to protect the children's eyes.

Demonstrate how to hold the nail between their thumb and forefinger, as well as the art of gently and steadily pounding on the nail. Use large nails so children have plenty of space to hold the nail and hit its head. The larger the better for young children. Roofing nails have wide flat heads (a little larger than a nickel) and make good targets. Until younger children have the steadiness and precision to hit the nail head and not their fingers, a rubber mallet-type hammer works nicely. In addition to the supreme satisfaction of making noise and accomplishing something meaningful, pounding nails is a great way to fulfill children's need for movement while also practicing hand-eye coordination skills.

THINKING

079
SEASHELLS BY THE SEASHORE

If you are fortunate enough to live near the ocean, collecting seashells and other interesting water artifacts (i.e., driftwood, sea glass, petrified wood) is a breeze. If you do not live by an ocean, there are many other ways to gather seashells: friends, family, parents, neighbors, and of course, there is always the dollar store or the Internet if you don't mind using man-made shells.

Once you have gathered a variety of seashells, there are so many ways to use them in the classroom:

- Categorizing by shape, species, or color.
  HINT: A silverware tray or muffin tin makes a nice and easy container to sort, categorize, and store the shells.
- Stringing a pattern of seashells on string lacing (be sure to find shells with holes for easy stringing).
- Seriating shells by size (from smallest to largest).
- Seashell match game. Gather at least a pair of about 5 to 6 different kinds of shells. Mix them up and place on a table for a small group of children to see. Pick up one shell and ask the children to find the shell(s) that match the one you are holding. Talk about the color, shape, and the shell's surface (i.e., rough, bumpy, smooth, or pointy). Once matched, set them aside. Pick up another shell and have the children help you find the matching one. Continue until all of the shells are matched.

NOTE: When collecting ocean treasures, be sure you do not harm a living creature by removing it from its home. If you do find a shell with an inhabitant, do not throw it back into the ocean as this can cause trauma (and even death). Instead, gently place the shell, open side down, on the ocean's sandy bottom.

Help children understand various concepts like opposites (big and little), sizes (long and short), or textures (smooth and rough) by giving them plenty of opportunities for classification and comparisons.

⊱ RECIPE ⊰
Seashell Clay

Beautiful paper weights or ornaments can be made with salt dough and a variety of seashells.

You will need:

- ☐ 2 cups flour
- ☐ 1 cup water
- ☐ 1 cup salt
- ☐ Seashells

Combine the flour and water together. After mixing thoroughly, add the salt, and then knead the dough to make it smooth. If you want colored dough, add a few drops of food coloring to the water before mixing. Allow the children to make whatever shapes they choose out of the dough and gently push the shells into the dough. Remind children to make a small hole in the object's top if it is going to be used as an ornament. Bake the little masterpieces in the oven at 200° F for 2 hours.

To find a seashell is to discover a world of imagination.
Michelle Held

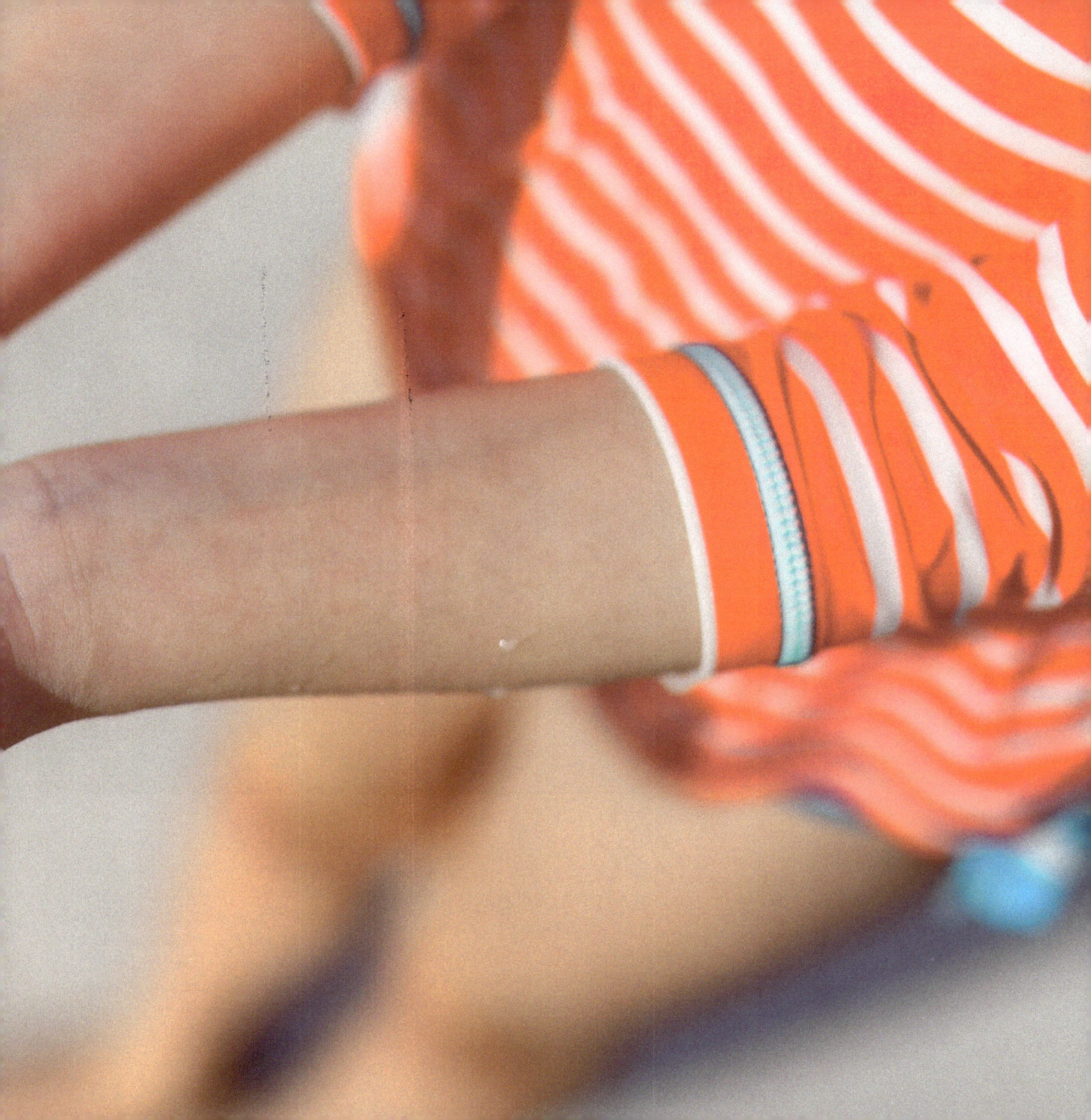

THINKING

080
ALPHABET SEASHELL MATCH

For this experience, the white clam shell works best. You will need two seashells for each letter of the alphabet. Mark the inside of one shell with the capital letter "A" and the inside of another shell with the lowercase "a." Continue in this fashion until you have a pair of seashells with an upper and lowercase for each letter of the alphabet. Place the seashells in an interesting wicker basket or wooden bowl. Children enjoy feeling the shells' textures while learning their upper and lowercase letters in an engaging and fun way!

081
SEASHELL JOURNALING

Older children enjoy researching and identifying shells by looking on the Internet or browsing through a seashell resource book. Once identified, it is fun to label the shells and perhaps record findings in a journal or on a chart. If you know where the shell came from (i.e., state, country) or what body of water it lived in (i.e., Pacific, Atlantic, Artic), it would be interesting to add these pieces of information to the documentation. Extend seashell journaling and investigation by encouraging children to bring in their collected shells from home and graph how many different types of shells the children have as a group.

Resource Guide

Seashells by Josie Iselin and Sandy Carlson

Shells: The Photographic Recognition Guide to Seashells of the World by S. Peter Dance

North American Seashells Poster by Feenixx Publishing

Encyclopedia of Shells by Kenneth Wye

THINKING

082

NATURE CONSTRUCTION: BUILDING IN A BIG WAY!

Children love building and construction. Given the time and materials, children will build as tall as they can, as wide as they can, as big as they can, and as complex as they can. When the block corner is filled with traditional items such as unit blocks, wooden people, and road signs, what you most likely get is some very traditional structures being built. However, when you provide large stones, bricks, sticks, and logs, a whole different architectural adventure happens with young children. The small walls and simple pathways are replaced with intricate structures such as homes, rivers, super highways, and bridges. Children's vocabulary increases with the addition of new and unique construction materials; cognitive problem-solving skills as well as gross motor skills are also challenged.

HINT: Gradually add natural elements to your block center so children are not overwhelmed with excitement, end up dumping more than they build, or use the materials in inappropriate ways. Add one or two new natural items each week so children are given the chance to incorporate these new elements into their building. They will anticipate something new, use it more effectively, and focus on it more intently if elements are introduced in small bits and pieces.

Using an old Chinese Checker board found at a resale shop, children cut small twigs and built their own forest.

Adding stones, bricks, twigs, and small logs infuses life into the block area—children's imaginations will soar with new and unique construction materials.

THINKING

RECIPE
Rainbow Fruit Skewers

083
COLOR SWATCH NATURE HUNT

Visit the local paint or decorating store and pick up a variety of paint swatches. With paint swatches in hand, go outside and look for the same colors in nature.

Be on the lookout for wildflowers, cattails, seagrass, or other interesting foliage growing by the roadside to collect and bring back to the classroom. Encourage children to match the foliage's color schemes to the color swatches.

Or, place collected nature in a vase. Place the vase in the art area along with the color swatches and similar colors of tempera paint so children might be encouraged to paint beautiful nature pictures.

These healthy fruit skewers are a simple and fun way for kids to explore colors even more!

You will need:

☐ Raspberries
☐ Tangerine segments
☐ Orange segments
☐ Pineapple chunks
☐ Kiwi fruit chunks
☐ Blueberries

Take wooden skewers and thread the following fruit onto each—1 raspberry, 1 tangerine segment, 1 orange segment, 1 chunk of peeled pineapple, 1 chunk of peeled kiwi, and finish off with 2 blueberries. Enjoy!

> *Look deep into nature, and then you will understand everything better.*
> **Albert Einstein**

PART FOUR

Sprouting

SPROUTING

All knowledge begins with wonder. Nature—with its infinite and boundless glory—is a kaleidoscope filled with wonder. Like a kaleidoscope, nature changes from moment to moment, revealing intricate patterns, dazzling colors, and magnificent feasts to our eyes, minds, and souls. Yet, for many of us, nature is so commonplace that we often don't hear the whip-poor-will's continuous chant and chatter, smell the wild mint growing by the roadside, or see spring's first tulip blooms. For some, it has been a long time (or maybe never) since we've messed about in the Earth's dirt, or even a bag of potting soil.

To explore the world of dirt is exhilarating for young children. They are fascinated by the feel and smell of dirt, and equally filled with a sense of wonder when tiny green sprouts appear from beneath its surface. Through this section, *Sprouting*, you will learn about ways to bring the outside world of seeds, plants, and gardens into your classroom. Instill nature's knowledge by offering children the wonder of growth and sprouting. It's time for you and your children to get your hands dirty and have the wondrous feel of dirt up to your elbows.

> What is a weed?
> A plant whose virtues
> have not yet been
> discovered.
>
> **Ralph Waldo Emerson**

SPROUTING

084
GROWING SUNNY SUNFLOWERS

Sunflowers make any day bright and cheery. Growing sunflowers is simple—even indoors. All you need are sunflower seeds, soil, a pot, water, and a dash of sunshine.

Grow sunflowers indoors in a few simple steps:

1. Find your sunflower seeds. There are lots of ways to get sunflower seeds such as asking around for a gardener who grows sunflowers. Your sunflower gardener could be the local nursery, gardening club, friends, family, colleagues, or even parents. Another way to get sunflower seeds is to locate wild sunflowers growing by the side of the road or in the alley behind the car repair shop. If all else fails, you can obtain sunflower seeds from the local nursery or garden center.

   HINT: Find seeds from dwarf sunflowers (i.e., Big Smile, Teddy Bear, or Pacino), so they won't quickly outgrow the classroom containers.

2. Gather pots or containers. Sunflowers aren't fussy, and will grow in most any type of container. However, sunflowers are avid growers so it is best to begin with a larger-sized container that is at least 16-inches in diameter and holds approximately 5-gallons of dirt. Examples of containers good for growing sunflowers include milk crates, window boxes, or large garden pots. If you are on a limited budget, ask others for cast-away pots or containers. You will be surprised what people find in their basements or garages.

3. Prepare your pots or containers. In the bottom of the pot, add a layer of drainage material such as rocks, seashells, or terra cotta pieces. Fill the pot with soil. Leave about 2-inches at the top of the pot so watering is easy.

4. Plant the seeds. Plant two seeds at a time about 1-inch deep and at least 3-inches apart. Place the containers in a very sunny spot in the classroom. Sunflowers need the sun's warmth for the greater part of the day. However, be careful that the spot is not too warm because extreme heat can damage the sunflower seeds and cause them not to grow.

   You don't have to wait long for a sunflower seed to sprout. Germination should happen in approximately 7 to 10 days. If the seeds do not sprout in 14 days, it is a sure sign that something must have happened in the germination process and they are not going to grow. This is a great lesson for young children. Did the sunflower seeds get too much water—or not enough water? Too little sun—or not enough sun? Was it too hot—or not hot enough?

5. Care for the sunny sunflowers. Sunny sunflowers require lots of water especially during the sprouting stage of growth. Be sure to keep the soil moist until the seeds sprout and then water on a regular basis. At some point, the sunflowers may become too large for their containers and should be transplanted to the great outdoors.

SPROUTING

085
EXPLORING SUNNY SUNFLOWERS

Find a sunflower plant for children to explore. If possible, have the whole flower to examine (i.e., seeds, flower head, leaves, stem, and roots). Place the plant on a table and allow children to discover the different parts of the sunflower. Cut a section off the bottom of the sunflower's stalk and begin a conversation with a small group of children about what the stalk looks like inside. Point out where the water is absorbed and discuss how the water travels up the stalk to the sunflower head. Magnifying glasses might be a nice addition for the children's explorations.

Once you have discussed the parts of the sunflower plant, consider these additional experiences to explore sunny sunflowers:

SEED SURPRISE
Encourage children to practice their fine motor skills by using tweezers or small tongs to pull the seeds from the plant and place in a container. Later, children can count or categorize the seeds.

SPROUTING

Or, place sunflower seeds in the sensory table along with other loose parts such as birdseed, sunflower leaves, and dirt. Sunflower seeds have interesting textures and shapes to explore.

SEED PENDANTS

Make pendants with sunflower seeds and a base such as cardboard. Provide cardboard circles about 2-inches in diameter with a hole punched in the top (older children can prepare the circles for the younger ones). Once children have plucked the seeds from the sunflower, glue the seeds onto the cardboard circle in any fashion they wish. Elmer's® Glue works great for this project. When the glue has dried, string some yarn or ribbon through the hole to create a beautiful sunflower pendant.

Another idea for the sunflower pendant base is to recycle old cardboard puzzle pieces. Punch a hole in the puzzle piece and then paint the front and back with black acrylic paint. Let the paint dry thoroughly and then glue sunflower seeds on one side of the puzzle piece. If making the pendant for a gift, you might want to spray with clear acrylic paint for a longer lasting piece of jewelry (adult job). String a ribbon or piece of twine through the hole, tie a knot, and place around your neck.

SUNFLOWER SKETCH

Place a sunflower in a large vase next to the painting easel and offer paints that are the colors of the plant (i.e., green, yellow, brown). Invite the children to paint a still life of the sunflower. An extension of this experience is to find books on Van Gogh's paintings—especially his famous sunflower series. Or, download images of Van Gogh's sunflowers, frame, and place by the real sunflower.

FEED THE BIRDS

Prepare a snack for the birds by arranging sunflower seeds on a piece of cardboard. Place in a bird feeder tray, on top of a fence post, or on a tree stump. You can also hang the whole sunflower head with some twine in a nearby tree. Blue Jays, Gold Finches and other birds will love to come and visit for a tasty sunflower seed snack.

SUNNY SNACKS

Sunflower seed snacks for children are fun and easy to make.

Here are three ideas:

- Spread cream cheese or mayonnaise on a piece of flatbread or English muffin. Use a cucumber slice for the center of the sunflower and then place the sunflower seeds around the cucumber slice to represent the flower's petals. Add some dill sprigs to represent the grass, and pop in your mouth to enjoy!

- Slice an apple into rings (you will need to remove the center core). Let children cover the apple ring with soy butter or cream cheese and then sprinkle shelled sunflower seeds on top for a crunchy, nutty flavor. Other items such as raisins or dried cranberries can be added for variety. Even though not nutritious, colored sprinkles give this tasty snack a fun and festive feel.

- Sunflower pita pockets are easy to make and good for you! Simply mix together cream cheese, grated carrots, raisins, and raw sunflower seeds. Stuff in a pita pocket. You could also use taco shells or tortillas for this healthy recipe.

Resource Guide

Big Yellow Sunflower by Frances Barry

Sunflower House by Eve Bunting

A Sunflower's Life by Nancy Dickmann

Sunflower by Miela Ford

This Is the Sunflower by Lola Schaefer

SPROUTING

086
CACTI CURIOSITY

Collect a variety of cacti and bring into the classroom for children to observe, compare, and contrast. Cacti provide amazing opportunities for pure observation because they are so incredibly varied and interesting. Invite children to notice the cacti's colors, sizes, textures, and leaves or spines. Offer books or pictures illustrating different kinds of cacti—especially those that may be prevalent in your area. A cacti garden is also fun to grow in the classroom. Once the cacti's basic needs are met (i.e., soil, sunny spot, small amounts of water), they do not need a lot of care and are fairly easy to grow.

Follow these steps to make your own cacti garden:

1. Purchase a few varieties of cacti from your neighborhood florist. Easy-to-grow varieties include Prickly Pear, Rebutia, or Rose Pincushion. Ask the florist for cacti suggestions and recommendations, and about their toxicity to humans and animals.

   NOTE: Do not purchase cacti with thin, clear prickles because if they poke into the body, they are very hard to remove, and also difficult to see.

2. Select a growing container for your garden. Shallow containers no more than 10-inches deep work best for growing cacti. Be sure the container has a drainage hole and tray for catching excess water.

   HINT: If the cacti turn brown, check to be sure you have good drainage.

3. Place a 1-inch layer of gravel or rocks on the bottom of the container and cover with a few inches of potting soil specifically designated for cacti. It is a misconception that cacti like a sand-based soil. Most cacti prefer rich and rocky soil.

4. With gloved hands, make a small indentation in the soil to place the cactus. Lightly press the cactus into the soil until it stands on its own. Then, add a few more inches of soil around the base of the cactus and gently press down the soil with your fingertips.

   HINT: If children's work gloves are not available, wrap a piece of newspaper around the cactus to protect children's hands and fingers.

5. Place a layer of gravel, small rocks, or sand on top of the potting soil and around the base of the cacti.

6. Fertilize using plant food with nitrogen and phosphorus. After the initial fertilizing, feed once or twice a year in the spring and summer. Be sure to keep fertilizer out of the reach of young children.

7. Find a sunny spot in the classroom where the cacti will receive 3 to 5 hours of sun each day.

   HINT: Warm sunny windowsills are the best places for cacti to not only grow, but positively thrive. If you need to relocate the garden to a different spot in the classroom, do so slowly by moving to the new spot for a few days, and then back to the old spot for a few days, and repeat for 1 or 2 months. This will allow the cacti to acclimate to their new home.

8. Water the cacti once a month in very small amounts. Rather than a watering can, use a measuring cup so you know exactly how much water is offered to the cacti garden. A rule of thumb is to slowly pour small amounts of water into the container and continue doing so until you see some water draining out into the container's tray. Check with your florist for recommendations on how much water is needed based on the size of your container and selected cacti.

SPROUTING

HINT: The easiest way to determine if the cacti garden needs water is to stick a finger about ½-inch into the soil. If the soil is dry, the garden needs watering. If the cacti turns yellow, use less water.

Young children are fascinated by cacti so they will enjoy caring for them. They are visually interesting and physically challenging, which encourages children's close observations and intense focus to ensure the safety of their fingers. Just make sure that little hands will not get pricked by having children wear thick work gloves when planting or watering. Here are a few fun experiences to engage children's curiosities in the cacti garden:

COMPARE & CONTRAST OBSERVATIONS

Invite children to compare and contrast the different varieties of cacti in the garden. Offer story and resource books containing images of cacti for children to learn about the life of a cactus. Children's observations of differences can be documented with drawings or photographs. Also, the number of blooms and plant growth can be documented or charted.

IDENTIFYING & LABELING

Encourage children to identify the kinds of cacti in the garden by reading books or researching on a Kindle or the Internet. After researching, children may enjoy labeling each variety.

CACTI ARTISTRY

Invite children to create cacti from clay and a variety of loose parts to represent the prickly needles such as toothpicks, sticks, thin wire, and paperclips.

CACTI EXPERIMENT

Purchase two identical cacti (size, width, height, and variety). Invite children to give each cactus a name (i.e., Sally, George) and to write the given names onto the cacti. Put one cactus in a sunny section of the classroom and the other in a place where there is little sunlight. Water the cactus in the sun as directed, but water the cactus in the little sunlight twice as often and twice as much as directed. Provide graph charts or documentation sheets for children to record the growth (or non-growth) of each cactus.

Resource Guide

Desert Giant: The World of the Saguaro Cactus by Barbara Bash

Deserts by Gail Gibbons

Cactus Hotel by Brenda Z. Guiberson

Cactus Cafe: A Story of the Sonoran Desert—A Wild Habitats Book by Kathleen Weidner Zoehfeld

CACTUS #1

PUT IN SUNNY, WARM PLACE

WATER MONTHLY

AMOUNT OF WATER AS DIRECTED

CACTUS #2

PUT IN LITTLE SUNLIGHT

WATER WEEKLY

2 TIMES THE AMOUNT OF WATER

NOTE: This is a long-term project, so everyone needs patience and persistency in conducting the cacti experiment!

SPROUTING

087
AIR PLANTS

If you don't have a green thumb, air plants are just for you! Air plants are epiphytes so they don't need to grow in soil. They just hang out anywhere you put them and thrive in bright light. Epiphytes suck nutrients out of the air so they are super easy to care for—just soak them in a bowl of clean water for 30 to 45 minutes each week and they will be happy as a lark in spring.

Air plants can be ordered online or purchased from a garden store or florist. Look for the variety of air plant called Tillandsia, which comes in numerous shapes and sizes. One easy idea is to attach the Tillandsia on a fishing line. Simply wrap a bit of the fishing line around the plant in between its leaves and then tie a double knot to secure in place on the line. Hang from the classroom's ceiling on a ceiling hook. Choose a place in the classroom where it can receive bright, but indirect light. A perfect place for hanging three or four lines of the Tillandsia garland is over the science corner.

To care for the Tillandsia garland, take off its hook twice a week and gently place into a sink or bucket filled with water for about 30 minutes. After carefully shaking the excess water from the garland, place on a paper towel to finish drying before rehanging. Between watering, the garland can be misted with water for an extra drink.

088
FASCINATING PODS

Tree pods are fascinating natural objects for young children. Seed pods come in a variety of shapes, sizes, and textures. For example, some tree pods are round and bumpy while others are round and flat. Some pods are leathery while others are smooth and shiny. There are seed pods with such conspicuous features that they become the distinguishing feature of the tree. Conversely, some tree pods are so small you barely notice them. Regardless of their physical characteristics, all tree pods hold one common fascination for children: What's inside?

Encourage children to discover the secrets of tree pods. The process of finding, observing, and opening seed pods helps children develop a respect for the diversity surrounding the natural world, and more importantly, discovering their secrets.

SEED PODS

HONEY LOCUST Red-brown pods approximately 7 to 10-inches long	**MESQUITE** Large, flattened pods streaked with red color
CAPE WATTLE Long, dark, bean-like pods	**MAPLE** Light-brown helicopter pods
CAROB Heavy, long, dark-brown pods	**KENTUCKY COFFEE** Thick, olive-brown pods
MIMOSA Long, brown, and bean-like pods	**ACACIA** Long, light-brown pods
CATALPA Immature pods are green; mature are brown, and 8 to 20-inches long	**REDBUD** Small, flat pods that change from green to purple in the fall
BLACK LOCUST Brown pods that remain attached to the tree in winter	**YELLOWWOOD** Bean-like, flat pods

It's early morning. Anthony is exploring the schoolyard. Kentucky coffee bean pods have fallen from the tree and are littering the lawn. "Look what I found!" He cries, scooping up a leathery seed pod. Soon Nada, Jamal, and Larissa are crowding around, gathering more and more pods in their hands. I find myself on the verge of launching into a set of pre-programmed "what" questions: What do you think is inside? What tree do you think they came from? But, somehow, I keep quiet, and Anthony, after several failed attempts figures out a way to break the thick pod apart to reveal a perfect little row of seeds nestled inside.

"Secrets," Anthony breathes. "Secrets," I breathe back, intensely grateful I have refrained from telling him something he has discovered for himself. Secrets is a far more descriptive word for what he has discovered, and besides, he has named the seeds, not me. "Let's find more secrets," he whispers.

Deb Matthews Hensley, "Discovering Science in Nature" *Scholastic Early Childhood Today,* May/June, 1999, 27-31.

> Your mind is a garden. Your thoughts are the seeds. You can grow flowers or you can grow weeds.
> **Ritu Ghatourey**

089
SEEDS GALORE

You can find seeds everywhere: on the ground outside, inside a fruit or vegetable, in a clear plastic bag at the grocery store, in the garden, in the woods, or inside the package of a dried soup mix. However, the easiest source for seeds is in the kitchen—either at home or in the early childhood center.

The kitchen can provide an endless supply of seeds for young children to explore. Most of the time, these seeds are leftovers from the preparation of our meals or snacks that usually find their way to the garbage can or compost pile. Why not save these seeds by creating a new home for them to sprout in some rich soil or a jar of crystal clear water? Since there are countless sizes, shapes, and kinds of seeds, why not find a place in the math area and use the seeds for counting, comparing, seriating, and classifying?

You can procure seeds by asking the center's cook for leftover seeds or soliciting the children to bring seeds their parents may have used in cooking or from a surplus in the kitchen cabinet. Collect and wash (if needed) the seeds. Invite children to explore the seeds with a magnifying lens and to touch and examine the seeds. Are they smooth, bumpy, hard, or soft? What colors are the seeds?

SEEDS FROM THE KITCHEN		
CANTALOUPES	PEARS	CHERRIES
PUMPKINS	PLUMS	MUSKMELONS
LEMONS	ORANGES	MANGOES
GRAPEFRUITS	SQUASH	APRICOTS
LIMES	CUCUMBERS	GRAPES
PEACHES	GREEN PEPPERS	POMEGRANATES
AVOCADOES	WATERMELONS	APPLES

RECIPE
Chia Seed Pudding

Continue children's seed discoveries with this fun recipe for a sweet and nutritious treat.

You will need:

- ☐ 2 cups milk
- ☐ ½ cup chia seeds
- ☐ ¼ cup unsweetened cocoa powder
- ☐ ¼ cup peanut or almond butter
- ☐ ½ teaspoon vanilla extract
- ☐ Toppings such as granola, fruit, or whipped cream (optional)

Add the milk, chia seeds, cocoa powder, peanut butter, and vanilla into a bowl and whisk until combined. Cover the bowl and place in the fridge overnight or for at least 4 hours. Add the pudding mixture to a blender and blend until smooth and creamy. Serve the chilled chia pudding to children in bowls or small jars with desired toppings.

SPROUTING

Seeds are wonderful natural elements for investigation. Here are a few fun ideas to get you started:

SEED SORTING & MEASURING

Provide children with bowls of seeds, beans, corn, and small seed pods along with measuring cups, spoons, and small tongs. Invite children to transfer the natural elements from one container to another by type, size, shape, or color. Examples of containers include muffin tins, silverware dividers, coconut halves, wicker baskets, and large clam shells. Are there seeds and beans that are the same color or size? How are they different? How many seeds does it take to fill one muffin cup? How many beans does it take? Is it easier to transfer the seeds using tongs or scooping with spoons?

SPROUTING

SEED PAINT

Add a variety of interesting seeds to the children's finger paint such as fennel, sesame, or poppy seeds and watch the interesting designs appear. Adding each specific seed to a contrasting color of finger paint helps children see and possibly identify the seeds in the paint. Poppy seeds (black in color) added to yellow paint, and sesame or fennel seeds (light in color) added to red paint helps highlight the actual seeds. Incorporating seeds into finger paint also creates the added dimension of texture to the paint, which enhances the kinesthetic experience.

Resource Guide

The Tiny Seed by Eric Carle

I Really Wonder What Plant I'm Growing by Lauren Child

Growing Vegetable Soup and *Planting a Rainbow* by Lois Ehlert

From Seed to Plant by Gail Gibbons

The Carrot Seed by Ruth Krauss

From Seed to Pear by Ali Mitgutsch

090
BEAN MOSAIC

Provide children with lids from jars or small plastic plates and a variety of dried beans or lentils. After children pour glue about ⅛-inch thick in the lid or plate, invite them to position the dried beans or lentils in a pattern of their choice. Allow the glue to dry overnight. To preserve the mosaic, spray the surface with a clear shellac when children are not in the classroom.

SPROUTING

091
CONTAINER GARDENS

Even if your classroom is located in a metropolitan area with little green space, you can still grow amazing gardens within the room's four walls. Container gardens do not need a large piece of land or even a lot of space—all you need is light, dirt, water, and a collection of containers for the plants. It is also not necessary to invest a lot of money in purchasing the containers. Take a look around your classroom, garage, basement, or even the center's kitchen for vases, bowls, vessels, mason jars, or even thick glass bottles. You might be surprised at the many cast-off objects that can be magically transformed into whimsical containers.

Container gardens thrive near sunny windows and on windowsills. Just give the cheerful gardens a drink of water when they are thirsty and an occasional dose of fertilizer (be sure to store fertilizer in a locked cabinet out of reach of children). Avoid placing the container gardens in spots that experience any blasts of cold or hot air. Because the gardens are positioned in the warm sun, they have a tendency to dry out rapidly so it is important to check daily for moisture. Young children love doing anything involving water, so this is a good responsibility for classroom helpers.

UNIQUE MINI-GARDEN CONTAINERS

HAT	BRICK (WITH HOLES)	TIN CAN
TUB	MASON JAR	CONCRETE BOWL
RUBBER BOOT	WATERING CAN	SUITCASE
DUMP TRUCK TOY	SMALL WAGON	HIGH-HEELED SHOE
WORK GLOVE	LARGE COFFEE CUP	TIN CUP
TIN BOX OR BUCKET	WICKER BASKET	SMALL WASTEBASKET
TIN PAIL	WOODEN BARREL	WHEELBARROW
CERAMIC BOWL	MUFFIN TIN	DRAWER
PAINT CAN	LARGE SEASHELL	PICNIC BASKET
TEA TIN	FISH BOWL	COLANDER
CINDERBLOCK	TEAPOT	GLASS BOTTLE
DRIED GOURD	GRAPEFRUIT HALF	FLAT-BOTTOMED PURSE

SPROUTING

Tips to Get Going on Growing Mini-Gardens:

- In the bottom of the container, to encourage proper drainage:
  - Punch a few ½-inch holes;
  - Place a layer of rocks; or
  - Place a layer of rocks and a thin mesh screen on top.

- Maintain a constant room temperature between 65 and 70°F.

- Line containers that may leak (i.e., colander, wicker basket) with a plastic bag, saran wrap, or aluminum foil.

- Use potting soil for best growing results.

- Select a spot in the classroom that receives at least 4 hours of natural sunlight. If more light is needed, purchase a small plant light and suspend it over the containers.

- Seedlings grown indoors may be susceptible to mildew. To prevent this, brew some chamomile tea and let cool. After the tea is cooled, water, spray, or gently spritz on the seedling plants.

Instead of throwing away that box of stale ice cream cones, recycle the cones into fun containers for plants. Start seeds such as basil or mint in cones, plant the cones in the ground, and watch your ice cream garden grow!

> We know we cannot plant seeds with closed fists. To sow, we must open our hands.
> **Adolfo Pérez Esquivel**

SPROUTING

092
INDOOR WATER GARDENS

If you have an aversion to dirt, then an indoor water garden may be just the thing for you. Water gardens are easy gardening projects for young children, and because most water gardens are in clear containers, they can easily see the root system. Simply find a clear container and layer a few black river rocks, marbles, beads, pebbles, or gravel on the bottom ¼ of the container. Black river rocks work terrific because of their colorful contrast with the green plants.

Pick an easy growing, non-toxic plant to put in the water bottle such as a spider plant, purple passion, coleus, amazon sword, or pennywort. Herbs are also well-suited to underwater growing. The following herbs are right at home in water: mint, basil, rosemary, sage, oregano, and lavender. If you are unsure about what plants grow best in water, visit your local florist or nursery. Most water plants are sold with a small wire or mesh basket encasing their root system. These baskets help to keep the roots underneath the rocks so be careful not to remove.

Carefully place the plant and its roots on top of the rocks, then cover the plant's roots with more rocks. Fill the container ¾ full with water. Unchlorinated, unfiltered water works best, but tap water also works just fine. Find a spot in the classroom without direct sunlight as the warm sun might promote algae growth. Every so often, put the container under the water faucet to slowly flush out the stale water and replace it with fresh water. Adding a plant aquatic fertilizer will also keep the plant healthy.

SPROUTING

093
NATURAL SPONGE GARDEN

Plant a fast-growing garden on a natural sponge. Soak the natural sponge in water for 10 to 15 minutes and then gently squeeze the excess moisture out of the sponge. After soaking some fast-growing seeds (i.e., mung beans, parsley, grass, mustard) in room temperature water for at least 4 hours, drop the seeds into the holes of the partially wet sponge. Tie a string around the sponge and hang it up in a moderately sunny spot. Check the sponge each day to be sure it is moist—a good responsibility for children and an excellent documentation opportunity. On the weekends, give the sponge an extra dose of water or place the sponge in a shallow container with a small amount of water to keep it from drying out.

094
HYDROPONIC GARDEN

What you need:

- ☐ Yogurt cup
- ☐ Small jar, slightly larger than the yogurt cup
- ☐ Plant
- ☐ Small rocks or pebbles
- ☐ Cotton wick like a strip of rope, T-shirt, or yarn

1. Poke a hole in the bottom of the yogurt cup.
2. Thoroughly wet the cotton wick.
3. Thread the wick through the hole in the yogurt cup.
4. Add water to the jar, place the yogurt cup on top of the jar, making sure that the wick is submerged in the water.
5. Fill the yogurt cup about ¼ full with small rocks or pebbles, gently place the plant in the yogurt cup.
6. Place the plant in a sunny spot and add water when the level gets low in the jar. For a healthier plant, add water-soluble nutrients to the jar.

SPROUTING

Find a narrow-mouthed clear container such as a mason or mayonnaise jar. Poke several toothpicks into the bottom ⅓ of the potato and suspend it over the jar. Fill the container with water until just the bottom part of the potato is submerged. Place in an area where children can observe the growing roots. Sweet potatoes grow easily in sunny places as well as darker spaces in the classroom. It doesn't take long for the thin white roots to appear and very quickly the jar will be filled with a maze of sweet potato roots. Soon, the sweet potato will begin sprouting leaves, and before you know it, a trail of vines will be traveling along your classroom's countertops.

Depending on the classroom's climate, the water can evaporate quickly so be sure to frequently check the water level. Also, be sure to give the sweet potato plant a fresh drink of water every few days. All you need to do is put the container under the water faucet, turn on the cool water, and run into the jar until clear water appears.

095
SWEET POTATO VINES

Go to the grocery store or local farmer's market to find a nice plump sweet potato. Look for a firm potato with no bruises on its outer skin. Because potatoes are sometimes sprayed with a growth inhibitor, be sure to thoroughly wash and scrub the potato's skin with a kitchen brush before allowing children to handle.

096
KITCHEN SCRAP GARDENS

In early spring, it is not atypical to see beans sprouting in early childhood classrooms either in egg cartons, small paper cups, or plastic Ziploc® bags hanging on the windows. Why not enlarge the children's gardening repertoire? Try growing bits and pieces of leftovers from the kitchen: avocado seeds, pineapple tops, sweet potatoes, carrot tops, and seeds from tomatoes, cucumbers, grapefruits, lemons, oranges, and limes.

With kitchen scrap gardens, you don't need a full-blown outdoor garden since these gardens can be grown inside the classroom. In some cases, kitchen scrap gardens don't even need dirt because water works just fine! The general rule for planting kitchen leftovers is to plant the seeds in dirt; and place the pits, tops, and bulbs in water.

In addition to the planting, watering, and general care of kitchen scrap gardens, these mini-gardens offer many possibilities for children's learning:
- Observation skills (observing growth and possibly non-growth of plants).
- Journaling experiences (writing and documenting the plant's growth progress).
- Mathematical concepts (measuring the height and predicting regrowth).
- Photography projects (photographing the plant's growing phases).

Here are some ideas to get you started:

PINEAPPLE
Fresh pineapple is a little taste of heaven. It's sweet, juicy, and succulent. Growing a pineapple takes patience and perhaps a little bit of luck.

Follow these steps:
1. Go to the grocery store (or in your backyard if you are fortunate to have a pineapple tree nearby) and find one without brown or yellow leaves. One test for a ripe pineapple is to tug on one of its leaves (the leaf should pull out easily). However, do not select an overly ripe pineapple because they are harder to grow.

NOTE: Be sure that the pineapple doesn't have scale insects (small, grayish spots), which are usually located at the base of the crown or under the leaves.

Back in the classroom, grasp the base of the pineapple's crown with one hand, and quickly twist, and pull off the top (prickly leaves) with the other hand. You may find this challenging for little hands, but with a little elbow grease, the top will pop right off.

SPROUTING

SPROUTING

2. Look at the pineapple's top and find the little yellow nub at the base of the crown. Pick off any extra pineapple flesh on the nub and pull off a few of the outer leaves to expose the stem. Be sure the nub and leaves stay together because this is where the root system will grow from.

3. Cut a few horizontal slices about ¼-inch deep into the nub. Hang the pineapple upside down in a cool spot to dry for about 3 days. Drying the nub and pineapple core is an important step, which allows the cut horizontal slices to dry out and make this area hard.

   NOTE: The nub area must be hardened before you go to the next step.

4. Locate a narrow-opening jar (i.e., mason) that is large enough for the pineapple's nub to be partially submerged in water. Poke a few toothpicks into the crown so you can suspend it on the edges of the jar's opening until the root system starts to develop and grows a few inches long. Be sure the water level is just up to the crown's nub and not completely submerged. Completely submerging the crown will cause rot and sure death to the pineapple crown.

HINTS:
- Change the water frequently to avoid rotting or mold.
- Place in a sunny spot in the classroom.
- Be careful about the plant being in either too hot or too cold of an environment.
- The water level of the container is most important so watch it carefully.

5. Once the pineapple crown has developed an adequate root system, it is time to find a permanent home for the plant. Choose a 6 to 8-inch diameter pot, approximately 7 to 8-inches deep, with a good drainage system.

6. To plant the pineapple, use a garden soil with 30% organic matter. Fill the pot halfway with soil and gently place the pineapple nub on top of the soil. Next, spoon soil on the top of the crown until it is covered. Press the soil down firmly, being sure not to get dirt on the pineapple's leaves. If dirt lands on the leaves, gently brush away. Pineapple plants love moisture and warmth so place the pot in a sunny spot in the classroom where temperatures do not drop below 65°F. If your classroom is dry, try misting the plant with a spray water bottle.

❧ RECIPE ☙
Pineapple Upside-Down Snack

Children enjoy cooking and especially eating what they cook so they will love making this delicious pineapple snack.

You will need:

- ☐ Pineapple chunks
- ☐ Sunflower seeds
- ☐ Raisins
- ☐ Cottage Cheese
- ☐ Small cups and plates

Provide a small cup for each child and encourage the children to place pineapple chunks, sunflower seeds, and raisins in the bottom of the cup. Spoon cottage cheese over the chunks, seeds, and raisins until the cup is filled to the top and press firmly into the cup. When ready to eat, invite children to place a small, non-breakable plate on top of the container and carefully flip over. Children now have a yummy upside-down treat to enjoy. Experiment with other fresh or dried fruits and granola or cereals to create more upside-down surprises.

SPROUTING

CARROT
Method #1:
1. Take a trip to the local farmer's market to find carrots with green tops (or go to the grocery store and buy carrots in bulk).

2. Bring the carrots back to the classroom and place in a clear container filled with water.

3. Find a sunny spot such as a window sill for the carrots to grow. Don't be disappointed if the carrots look a little unhealthy and droopy at first. After a week or so, they should perk up and begin to grow new feathery green tops.

4. To keep the carrots healthy, be sure to change the water every week.

Method #2:
1. Cut 1-inch up from the main part of the carrot.

2. Insert the carrot into soil with the cut side down and leave about ½-inch of the other end of the carrot above the soil.

3. Water and place in a cool, but sunny spot in your classroom. It may take several weeks for regrowth to happen. Watch for tiny sprouts popping out from the top of the carrot.

CELERY
1. Cut the base (or bottom) part off from the celery stalks and rinse.

2. Place in a small cup of warm water, put on a sunny windowsill, and wait for the celery to grow—you should see new growth in approximately 10 days. Be sure to clean the water frequently.

3. Once there is significant growth (3 to 5 months), it is easy to transplant the plant either to an indoor container or outside in the warm garden.

SPROUTING

LETTUCE

1. The next time you make Caesar salad for dinner, save the very bottom or heart of the head of romaine or iceberg lettuce.

2. Simply place the lettuce core in a small container with about ½-inch of water in the bottom.

3. Every other day, keep the water fresh by changing it out. Then, all you have to do is wait for new leaves to begin growing in the center of the lettuce's heart.

GREEN ONIONS
Method #1:

1. Either pull green onions up from your garden, visit a farmer's market to find onions with roots, or go to the grocery store.

   NOTE: Finding green onions with roots is the hardest part of this project.

SPROUTING

2. Once found, drop the onions with roots pointing down in a container with 1-inch of water. Rinse and refresh the water every few days.

Method #2:

1. Cut 1-inch up from the bulb (or bottom of onion). Be sure to leave the roots intact.

2. Insert the bulb root side down into the soil and leave about ½-inch of the other end of the onion above the soil.

3. Water and place in a cool, but sunny spot in your classroom. It will take about 2 weeks for regrowth to happen. The green onions create a wonderful earthy aroma in your classroom.

CUCUMBER

Children will love how easy it is to grow cucumbers from seeds, and after they have grown them, they will be delicious in salads and fun to use in dips!

Follow these steps:

1. Save the seeds from the center of a cucumber when using it for snack or lunch. You will want to wash the seeds off and dry on a paper towel.

2. Plant one seed about ½-inch deep per section of a seedling tray or paper cup. You can either make a hole in the dirt and drop the seeds into it, or you can place the seeds on top of the soil and gently press them in.

3. Since seedlings grow so fast, they will quickly outgrow the seedling trays, so it's a good idea to transfer them to a large pot. You could also use a plantable peat pot that can later be placed in an outdoor garden.

4. After you're done planting the cucumber seeds, show the children how to water them well, and soon you'll see the cucumber seedlings popping out of the dirt.

5. Since cucumbers grow so fast, you can have the children plant the seedlings directly into a garden after all chance of frost is gone in the spring.

Cucumbers can be grown anywhere from full sun to part shade, but the more sun they get, the better they will produce.

6. Cucumbers are best harvested before they get too large. If they grow too large they tend to have lots of seeds in them.

7. The next step is talking to the children about how they would like to enjoy the cucumbers. Will they use them in a salad, make cucumber slices for dipping, or make dill pickles? Whatever they decide, it will make a healthy and yummy snack!

> *The glory of gardening: hands in the dirt, head in the sun, heart with nature. To nurture a garden is to feed not just the body, but the soul.*
> **Alfred Austin**

If a child is to keep alive his inborn sense of wonder without any such gift from the fairies, he needs the companionship of at least one adult who can share it, rediscovering with him the joy, excitement and mystery of the world we live in.
Rachel Carson

097
WHIMSICAL MUSHROOM FAIRY GARDEN

Young children love fairy gardens—they are fanciful and filled with imagination and playful thoughts. Create an enchanting fairy garden filled with whimsical mushrooms made from wine corks (for stems) and sea shells (for caps). Children will enjoy gluing the caps and stems together using a liquid glue such as Elmer's® and then painting the seashell caps with acrylic or tempera paint. To prevent smearing, be sure to seal the paint with clear acrylic spray.

Now the fun begins! Offer children opportunities to design the fairy garden by letting them decide its location such as adjacent to the walkway outside, in the classroom's sensory table, or the center's entryway. Place a thin layer of dirt on the bottom of the container and then place a layer of alfalfa seeds on top of the dirt. Cover the seeds with another thin layer of potting soil. Add earthworms or grass seed for additional interest to the fairy garden. Place the mushrooms in the garden and gently water—wait a few days—and watch the sprouting and fun begin!

SPROUTING

098
THE GRASS IS ALWAYS GREENER

Welcome children to plant different varieties of grass in small shallow bins. Place the bins side-by-side on a window sill or sunny spot in the classroom. Be sure to water the grass seeds based on what the directions say (a great job for children). It might be interesting to create a growth chart on a piece of tag board and measure the grass growth over a period of 2 weeks. Also, close observations of the characteristics of grass might enhance children's observations by asking questions like: Which grass is higher? Which grass is thicker? Which grass is greener?

Prior to planting, invite children to look at the packages of grass seed and talk about the differences they see—children may notice variation in the texture, height, and color of the grasses. Encourage children to hypothesize about how the grass they planted might look when grown.

Don't forget to cut the grass with children! Some terrific places for grass cuttings include the block corner to add to creative construction; the math area for counting, measuring, and seriation activities; or the dramatic play area as the noodles in child-made soup.

SPROUTING

099
CHARMING CHERRY TOMATO

Gardening is a very gratifying experience for children. Depending on their age, children enjoy gardening in different ways. Toddlers and young preschoolers love the sensory experience of playing in the wonderful dirt, feeling and exploring the fascinating seeds, and of course, using the water hose. Older children are more interested in understanding how a single, tiny seed turns into a plant and produces something to eat. Regardless of age, offering children opportunities to be a part of the growing process certainly impacts how they embrace tasting and eating what they have grown.

One of the easiest garden crops to grow is cherry tomatoes. The cherry tomato plant is relatively small so you can place it in a sunny spot on the play yard out of the pathway of balls, bikes, and active children. When planting the tomato seeds or young tomato plants, make sure the soil is warm. Seeds will not germinate and grow in cold soil. Gently water, being careful not to overwater and drown the seeds or seedlings.

Once the tomato plant's growth has taken off, pinch off the lower leaves so the plant will stay strong on the bottom to support the weight of the tomatoes. Tomato plants need a sturdy support to keep them growing tall and staying healthy. Use a bamboo stick, small tree branch, tomato cage, or trellis for supporting the plant. Be sure to watch out for bugs (i.e., aphids, spider mites) that love the tasty tomato plant's leaves. If you see signs of spiders or aphids, wash the leaves with soapy water to knock off the bugs so they won't eat the leaves that support the plant.

Bring the cherry tomato garden experience inside. Talk with the children and decide what they would like to grow in the classroom. Maybe they really like the cherry tomatoes and want to continue growing them—or maybe they would like to try growing something new. Try growing plants indoors because children are typically fascinated with the growing process whether it's indoors or out.

SPROUTING

RECIPE
Cherry Tomato Jam

What child doesn't like jam? Even children who are not crazy about the taste of fresh tomatoes might be willing to sample some sweet and delicious cherry tomato jam. Cherry tomato jam is similar to ketchup and tastes great on children's favorites such as tater tots or French fries, hot dogs or hamburgers, and scrambled eggs.

To make cherry tomato jam, use cherry tomatoes grown from your classroom or parent's garden, farmer's market, or grocery store. This is a good opportunity to have a conversation about all the foods we eat and enjoy that are made using tomatoes (i.e., ketchup, spaghetti sauce, and finely chopped in salsa).

What you need:

- ☐ 8 cups cherry tomatoes
- ☐ 2 cups sugar
- ☐ 1 tablespoon cinnamon
- ☐ 1 tablespoon cloves
- ☐ 2 teaspoons salt
- ☐ Crockpot

1. Chop tomatoes in half with plastic knives (children's job). Don't worry if the tomatoes get squishy with little hands—they are going to cook down anyway and you won't be able to tell the difference.

2. Measure remaining ingredients (children's job).

3. Place all ingredients into cold crockpot (children's job).

4. Turn crockpot on low (adult job).

5. Cook jam in the crockpot on low heat for approximately 4 hours or until tomatoes melt down and mixture is jam-like (crockpot's job). Take jam out of the crockpot and put in bowl (adult job) and let rest until cool.

6. Enjoy the sweet delicacy (everyone's job).

Sketching cherry tomatoes—and sampling a few—is quite a tasty treat!

SPROUTING

100
FARMER'S MARKET FUN

Visiting the farmer's market or neighborhood community garden is fun. It is one of the best places for young children to learn about the many different types of vegetables and making healthy food choices. Going to the community farmer's market is like having the farm come right to your backdoor. Because farmer's markets reflect the growing seasons, there is always something new to see, learn about, and even taste. Cooking up a tasty treat with something purchased at the farmer's market will inspire those finicky eaters to try something new. Or, finding some herbs and making bouquets infuses wonderful aromas and brings natural beauty into the classroom. Here are some ideas to get you started:

VEGETABLES, VEGETABLES

Walk around the farmer's market and let the children pick out a variety of vegetables. Ask them to find a vegetable that is long and thin—or small and round. Find a vegetable that comes in bunches, stalks, or heads. Talk about the vegetable's surfaces: Is it smooth? Bumpy? Prickly?

When you bring the fresh vegetables back to the classroom, provide opportunities to weigh, measure, or classify. Place the vegetables in the home living center for children to wash. Or, prepare the vegetables for a nutritious snack!

HERB BOUQUETS

In the summertime, herbs are commonplace at the farmer's market where you can find rosemary, basil, sage, lavender, or lemon verbena, to name a few. Back in the classroom, spread the herb branches out on a work surface and arrange small bouquets. Trim the stems of the herbs if they are different lengths, and tie each bouquet with a ribbon or piece of twine. Now comes the most fun: finding the perfect place for the herb bouquets.

There are lots of terrific places:
- Hung above the table in the home living area.
- Placed in a vase by the sink in the children's bathroom.
- Poked in a lump of clay and put in the block area to represent bushes and trees.
- Used as a paintbrush at the art easel.
- Placed in a small wicker basket by the sign in/out area for parents to enjoy (and smell).

SPROUTING

PESTO POSSE

The farmer's market is just the place to find fresh basil, and it is pretty inexpensive if you buy in late summer when the growth season is at its peak. One of the best things to make from fresh basil is pesto, which is a perfect sauce for spaghetti noodles.

You will need:

- ☐ 3 cups basil leaves
- ☐ 2 tablespoons pine nuts
- ☐ 1 clove garlic
- ☐ 2 tablespoons fresh lemon juice
- ☐ ½ cup extra-virgin olive oil
- ☐ ¼ cup grated Parmesan cheese

Place all ingredients in a blender and pulse until smooth (adult job). Store in an airtight container in the refrigerator, which will keep for up to 10 days. Toss with freshly cooked spaghetti noodles.

HINT: Children can help with this cooking project by measuring ingredients, tearing the basil leaves from the stems, rinsing the basil, and squeezing the lemon juice. If you have a mortar and pestle, they will enjoy crushing the garlic and salt together to make a paste, as well as pounding the basil leaves and nuts until they make a paste. Then, add all of the ingredients to a bowl and whisk or place in a blender and pulse until smooth.

BASIL CATERPILLARS

Enjoy making, and then eating, basil caterpillar salads made with cherry tomatoes and mozzarella for the head; ripe olives for the eyes and mouth; and fresh basil sprigs for the caterpillar's leaf.

GREEN SMOOTHIE

You will need:

- ☐ 2 cups milk
- ☐ 3 handfuls of spinach leaves, baby kale, or Swiss chard
- ☐ 2 cups strawberries, apples, pineapple, or peaches
- ☐ 1 avocado
- ☐ 1 banana
- ☐ 2 tablespoons chia seeds, flax seeds, or coconut oil
- ☐ 1 tablespoon vanilla extract
- ☐ 1 to 2 tablespoons maple syrup or honey (optional)
- ☐ ½ teaspoon cinnamon or nutmeg (optional)
- ☐ 1 handful of ice cubes

1. Tear the leaves into pieces.
2. Place all ingredients in a blender and blend on medium for approximately one minute.
3. Pour into glasses to serve.

Children can help:

- Rinse and dry spinach, baby kale, or Swiss chard leaves and remove stems.
- Peel avocado with fingers.
- Peel banana and cut into pieces.
- Measure out remaining ingredients.
- Help blend the smoothie.

Resource Guide

Green Smoothie Magic and *I Love Greens* by Victoria Boutenko

What's Wrong with Pajarraco? by Francisco Fernández del Castillo

I Will Never Not Ever Eat a Tomato by Lauren Child

The Boy Who Loved Broccoli by Sarah A. Creighton

Picky Eater by Michael Gordon

Monsters Don't Eat Broccoli by Barbara Jean Hicks

The Seven Silly Eaters by Mary Ann Hoberman

Gregory, the Terrible Eater by Mitchell Sharmat

Eat Your Veggies, Goldilocks: A Story about Healthy Eating by Steve Smallman

Picky Micky: The Boy Who Thought New Food Was Icky Icky! by Tiffany A. Smith

The Giant Green Lettuce Head: The Story about the Importance of Eating Salad by Maria Thompson

The Unpopular Pea (& Carrot) by Elle Valentine

SPROUTING

101
DANDY DANDELIONS

In many parts of the country, dandelions are abundant—much to the chagrin of folks who consider them a nuisance and eyesore to their manicured lawns. Remember your childhood, and putting a dandelion under your chin to make it appear yellow, giving a bouquet to that very special person, and blowing puffs of dandelions to the wind. Remember.

For young children, dandelions are magical and offer many hours of imaginative play and experiences. Just gathering this whimsical yellow flower is exhilarating for children and equally so for the adult when they are presented with a sweet dandelion bouquet. So, stop thinking of dandelions as a nuisance and begin thinking of them as an opportunity for children to explore and delight in their magic. Here are some ideas to get you started:

DANDELION HUNT
Take a nature walk around the playground, park, or down the sidewalk. It won't take long to find these cheerful little weeds. Look for a variety of dandelions in their different stages of growth: green buds with the flower not yet open; bright yellow flowers; and those that have gone to seed dressed in their puffy whites. Bring the dandelions back to the classroom for closer observations and help children to compare and contrast the differences in the found dandelions.

NOTE: If dandelions are collected in an area that may have been sprayed with weed chemicals, douse them in a mixture of cold water and a small amount of white vinegar. Remind children never to eat anything from nature unless an adult approves.

DANDELION PRINTS
The dandelion's physical shape makes unique little prints on paper that almost look like paint splats. First, collect dandelions on a beautiful spring day. Next, invite children to dip the dandelion flower into yellow paint (tempera paint works great) and press gently on a piece of paper.

DANDELION BOUQUETS
Challenge children to collect a bunch of dandelions—both yellow and white for a special bouquet. Turn a colander upside down and encourage children to poke the found dandelions in the colander's holes in whatever pattern they choose. When all of the colander's holes are filled, place the beautiful bouquet in the classroom for all to enjoy.

DANDELION PAINTBRUSHES
Store away your ordinary brushes and create something extraordinary with dandelion paintbrushes. Clip the base of the dandelion to a pinch clothespin and paint away!

HINT: Use thinned tempera paint and encourage children to be gentle as they dip the dandelion in the paint and apply to the paper. Doing so will produce wispy-like beautiful paintings.

DANDELION DYE
Challenge children to find and pick about 50 dandelions and place in a pot with enough water for the dandelions to float on top. Bring to a boil, reduce heat, and simmer for about 1 hour (adult job). Simmering the dandelions will make the water turn a dark brownish color. Let the water cool and then help children separate the dandelions from the water with a sieve.

There are several ways to use the dandelion dye:
- Put white muslin or cotton material into the brownish-colored dye for 3 hours. The white material will turn a dandelion-yellow color.

SPROUTING

- When making play dough, replace regular water with the dandelion dye.
- Add a little bit of the dandelion dye to white tempera paint and see what happens.

DANDELION PRESSING

Take children on a dandelion hunt to find the "bestest" dandelion in the bunch. Once each child has found their favorite dandelion, bring them back to the classroom. Put the dandelions between wax paper sheets and place in the pages of a large hardcover book. Close the book and put something heavy on top (i.e., rocks, cement brick, other large books). Within 10 days, the dandelions will be sufficiently pressed and can be carefully removed. Mount the pressed dandelions onto cardboard, old ceiling tile, or a piece of ceramic tile. Absolutely the "bestest!"

Dandelion Soufflé

After the dandelions in your lawn have gone to seed, shake their fluffy tops into an empty frozen pie pan until it is brimming over. Set in a moderate oven that is out of the wind. While it is cooking, seat your doll at a table located in a light breeze. Serve the soufflé immediately, and just watch it disappear! You will never have leftovers with this dish.

– From *Mud Pies and Other Recipes* by Marjorie Winslow

Resource Guide

The Dandelion Seed and *The Dandelion Seed's Big Dream* by Joseph Anthony

A Dandelion's Life (Nature Up Close) by John Himmelman

The Dandelion's Tale by Kevin Sheehan

SPROUTING

☙ RECIPE ☙
Dandelion Pancakes

Dandelions are a nutritious edible and can be made into tasty dishes including soups, salads, pancakes, and pancake syrup. The following is a recipe for dandelion pancakes.

You will need:

- ☐ 6 cups prepared dandelion flowers (see below hints for preparing flowers)
- ☐ ⅔ cup all-purpose flour
- ☐ ⅔ cup cornmeal
- ☐ 2 teaspoons baking soda
- ☐ 1 teaspoon salt
- ☐ 1 teaspoon ground cinnamon
- ☐ 1 teaspoon ground nutmeg (optional)
- ☐ ½ teaspoon ground cloves (optional)
- ☐ 2 eggs
- ☐ 1 cup milk
- ☐ 2 tablespoons honey
- ☐ Cooking or olive oil

1. Mix all dry ingredients together except the dandelion flowers. Add the eggs, milk, and honey to the dry mixture. Blend with a whisk, fork, or electric mixer until all the lumps have disappeared (children's job).

2. Pull apart the dandelion flowers from their stems and brackets; gently mix into the batter (children's job).

   NOTE: Brackets are found under the flowers at the top of their stems.

Brackets resemble a pod and have small leaves. Although brackets are not harmful to eat, they are bitter. What should go into the batter is just the yellow dandelion petals.

3. Warm oil in an electric frying pan and pour small puddles of batter into the pan (adult job). When batter bubbles appear on top of the pancake, flip over and cook for another few minutes until brown (adult job).

4. Serve warm with butter and syrup or fruit jelly (children and adult's job).

HINTS:

- The best tasting dandelions are found in early spring when they first appear on the landscape.

- The best time to harvest dandelions is mid-morning on a sunny day when the flowers are fully opened.

- Harvest in an area that has not been sprayed with chemicals and frequented by cats or dogs.

- There are other flowers that resemble the dandelion so make sure you are harvesting true dandelions. Go to the Internet and search how to identify the dandelion from other flowers or weeds, and you will find plenty of information about the characteristics of dandelions (i.e., dandelions' leaves are smooth without any fuzzy hairs).

When you look into a field of dandelions, you can either see hundreds of weeds or hundreds of wishes.

The journey of creating nature-based classroom experiences is YOUR unique and inspiring adventure. The journey of interacting with natural elements is the children's unique and inspiring adventure!

CONCLUSION

An Invitation to Extend the Journey

Young children love to explore and learn about the world around them. When children find interesting or meaningful objects to investigate, children inherently want to know more. You may want to create opportunities for intensive investigations or explorations around the experiences in this book that they are particularly enthusiastic about. Teachers Lycel Arboleda, Melanie Vega, Monique Heeg, and the children of the ISMILE Alam Atelier School in Indonesia did just that when they extended experience **030 Japanese Gyotaku (Fish Painting)** and documented their discoveries in "The Fish Journey."

Lively conversations and discussions, interesting play experiences, compelling questions, and wonderful opportunities to express their ideas emerged from this extended project. Children used simple representation to organize, record, and communicate mathematical concepts and scientific ideas. Through the Japanese Gyotaku, they learned to inquire, investigate, and solve problems while making decisions and choices to carry out and complete a task. The fish painting project was also about using their small muscles while learning to use tools and materials to take apart, assemble, invent, and construct.

CONCLUSION

So much learning was involved when the children decided to extend the art of fish painting and "rebuild" the fish.

Embark on a journey with your own children, and encourage extended investigations, discussions, questions, predictions, and presentations about an experience in which they show enthusiasm and interest. The following story told by the teachers at Alam Atelier will help you get started.

The Fish Journey
The children at Alam Atelier had been working on a project called Water Warriors for quite some time. The project included not only investigating different sources of water, but also examining concepts and theories about whales, sharks, fish, recycling, tsunamis, finding water sources, and even Bali beaches. The Gyotaku Experience—which is what the teachers started calling it—provided our children another language to showcase all these new concepts and ideas acquired through months of self-initiated research and investigation. It also gave them an opportunity to discover the external features of a fish in a sensorial and visual way. Through close observation, physically handling, and many conversations, children learned about the fish's scales, fins, eyes, and other parts of its anatomy.

A community decision was made to extend the Gyotaku Experience. Children began by intensely investigating the body of the fish that

CONCLUSION

had been placed on the table. They made visual illustrations of each body part of the fish they discovered. It was interesting to note the differences in their illustrating skills and how much detail each child retained and represented from their initial investigation of the fish.

Prior to dissecting the fish, the children decided it needed to be cooked. They preferred to dissect a cooked fish because they believed a cooked fish did not give out a very strong smell compared to the raw fish. This was an observation that stuck with the children and made them reconsider their schemas about fish. Zavier, for example, had been fishing and informed others that "Raw fish always smelled and they're not good for eating unless you cook them." Another child, Roby, said, "That's why we cook fish because they're smelly. Otherwise, no one will eat them."

After dissecting most of the fish, children ended up with an array of fish bones. Zavier noticed that the number of bones were not equal. He asked, "How come there's more bones on the right than here on the left?" Roby responded, "I think it's because there are some things over here like the guts. All fishes have guts."

"It looks very creepy." –Andie, 4 years

"The fish bones is fluffy." –Roby, 8 years

CONCLUSION

"The fish is broken." –Arseniy, 5 years

"Be gentle with the fish bones or else it can be broken." –Oliver, 6 years

A community decision was made to extend the Gyotaku Experience even more and to use various materials to "rebuild" the fish. Materials were presented to the children along with the question, "What can we do with these?" Given their knowledge of clay and how it is manipulated, children used clay to recreate the fish using its bones as the base. It was amazing to see how much the children remembered about the details of the fish and how much detail they were willing and wanted to include in their work. The teachers marveled at how resourceful the children were when they are fully motivated.

"The dorsal fin has straight lines on it. These details are the scales. Should be lots. Feel my scales. It's rough." –Roby, 8 years

CONCLUSION

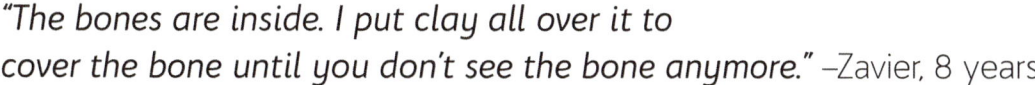

"There's actually fins also on the bottom part of the fish. It makes the fish swim a lot better."
–Oliver, 6 years

"I will make a pattern. It's dot, line, dot, line."
–Zavier, 8 years

"The bones are on the clay! Look!"
–Maikah, 8 years

"The bones are inside. I put clay all over it to cover the bone until you don't see the bone anymore." –Zavier, 8 years

"The fish bone makes it easier to make the fish." –Andie, 4 years

"I made a big fish." –Arseniy, 5 years

"My fish should be fat. It needs a lot of clay." –Talitha, 6 years

It was a great surprise seeing the children's representations of the fish. The children's striking works of art prove that they are all capable of making unique masterpieces even when they are all working on a similar project. The children's motivation came from an authentic interest in fish and other sea creatures. Gyotaku and the subsequent experiences provided a language for them to express their learning. It was amazing to witness their conversations peppered with the terms they read and researched about fish.

CONCLUSION

A Worthwhile Journey

Connecting young children with the natural world is an important responsibility for early childhood educators. Children who regularly have positive interactions with nature, as demonstrated by the Fish Journey, experience significant benefits such as increased abilities to concentrate, improved powers of observation, enhanced creativity, and advanced fine motor coordination and physical fitness. Although these benefits are critical to young children's growth, the greatest benefit of interacting with nature is the development of a sense of wonder. According to early childhood experts, a sense of wonder is the most important motivator for life-long learning, and isn't this our ultimate goal as early childhood educators—to provide worthwhile experiences that foster young children's love for learning?

Young children have a strong disposition to discover and explore their world—both outside and inside. They love to interact and connect to their immediate environment through hands-on, open-ended, and sensory-oriented experiences. This book encourages you to provide these types of experiences for the children in your classroom. It is important to understand, however, that everything begins outside—one must journey outside in order to be able to bring nature inside.

Bringing nature into your classroom isn't about reaching an ultimate and final destination.

CONCLUSION

It isn't about following rules, copying ideas, or being exact and finite. It isn't about finishing tomorrow, the next day, the next month, or even in a school year. It is about discovering simple ways you can bring nature inside—viewing the world from a new lens of always being on the lookout for natural elements you can gather from your local community—surrounding the classroom with beautiful natural elements—rediscovering yourself and all the children in your classroom. It is truly a worthwhile journey.

Begin the journey now.

Index

A

Acorns
- Acorn Adventure, 062
- Balancing Nature, 063
- Can You Estimate?, 071
- Creating Mandalas, 044
- Funny Nature Faces, 048
- Natural Loose Parts, 060
- Nature Artistry, 043
- Shake a Shrub, 003
- Sorting Bonanza, 061
- Treasure Tubs, 026

B

Bark
- Branch Weaving, 031
- Natural Loose Parts, 060
- Nature Artistry, 043
- Painted Tree Bark, 040
- Treasure Tubs, 026
- Tree Cookie Weaving, 032
- Using Natural Dyes for Ink, 073
- Writing With Nature, 072

Beans
- Balancing Nature, 063
- Bean Mosaic, 090
- Can You Estimate?, 071
- Funny Nature Faces, 048
- Musical Maracas, 045
- Natural Loose Parts, 060
- Sorting Bonanza, 061
- Treasure Tubs, 026

Birds
- Bird Nests, 053
- Bird Watching Art, 050
- Gourd Birdhouses, 052
- Milk Jug Bird Feeder, 051

Bricks
- Container Gardens, 091
- Nature Construction: Building in a Big Way!, 082
- Pretty Bricks, 056

Bugs
- Beauty of Spiderwebs, 015
- Insect Inspectors, 021
- Loving Ladybugs, 012
- Monarch Marvels, 005
- Nature or Not?, 027
- Pond Jars, 002
- Shake a Shrub, 003
- Worm Hotel, 022

C

Classroom Gardens
- Air Plants, 087
- Cacti Curiosity, 086
- Charming Cherry Tomato, 099
- Container Gardens, 091
- Hydroponic Garden, 094
- Indoor Water Gardens, 092
- Kitchen Scrap Gardens, 096
- Natural Sponge Garden, 093
- Sweet Potato Vines, 095
- The Grass is Always Greener, 098
- Whimsical Mushroom Fairy Garden, 097

Classroom Pets
- Adopt a Fish, 024
- Aquaponics Fun, 023
- Frisky Frogs, 013
- Geckos, 014
- Hermit Crabitats, 006
- Slug Bug B&B, 020
- Worm Hotel, 022

D

Dirt
- Cacti Curiosity, 086
- Charming Cherry Tomato, 099
- Container Gardens, 091
- Delicious Dirt, 041
- Growing Sunny Sunflowers, 084
- Natural Loose Parts, 060
- Pond Jars, 002
- Texture Walk, 007
- The Grass is Always Greener, 098
- Treasure Tubs, 026
- Whimsical Mushroom Fairy Garden, 097
- Worm Hotel, 022
- Writing With Nature, 072

Displaying Nature Collections, 029

Documenting Explorations, 028

Driftwood (see Twigs)

E

Explorer's Kit, 001

F

Fish
- Adopt a Fish, 024
- Aquaponics Fun, 023
- Japanese Gyotaku, 030
- Papier Mache, 054

Flowers
- Branch Weaving, 031
- Ceiling Tile Flower, 055
- Color Swatch Nature Hunt, 083
- Creating Mandalas, 044
- Dandy Dandelions, 101
- Exploring Sunny Sunflowers, 085
- Funny Nature Faces, 048
- Growing Sunny Sunflowers, 084
- Natural Loose Parts, 060
- Nature Artistry, 043
- Nature or Not?, 027
- Nature's Spirals, 033
- Potpourri, 058
- Shake a Shrub, 003
- Treasure Tubs, 026
- Tree Cookie Weaving, 032
- Using Natural Dyes for Ink, 073
- Wildflower Perfume, 059
- Wildflower Pounding, 057
- Writing With Nature, 072

Fruit
- Charming Cherry Tomato, 099
- Comparing Corn, 019
- Container Gardens, 091
- Farmer's Market Fun, 100
- Funny Nature Faces, 048
- Kitchen Scrap Gardens, 096
- Nature Artistry, 043
- Ok Okra!, 047
- Painting With Kitchen Scraps, 049
- Playing With Pumpkins & Gourds, 025
- Seeds Galore, 089
- Using Natural Dyes for Ink, 073
- Very Berry Berries, 018
- Writing With Nature, 072

G

Gardens *(see Classroom Gardens)*

Gourds
- Container Gardens, 091
- Funny Nature Faces, 048
- Gourd Birdhouses, 052
- Musical Maracas, 045
- Natural Loose Parts, 060
- Playing With Pumpkins & Gourds, 025

Grass
- Branch Weaving, 031
- Creating Mandalas, 044
- Funny Nature Faces, 048
- Natural Loose Parts, 060
- Nature Artistry, 043
- Texture Walk, 007
- The Grass is Always Greener, 098
- Tree Cookie Weaving, 032
- Using Natural Dyes for Ink, 073
- Writing With Nature, 072

H

Herbs
- Container Gardens, 091
- Farmer's Market Fun, 100
- Herb Hullabaloo, 010
- Indoor Water Gardens, 092
- Natural Loose Parts, 060
- Using Natural Dyes for Ink, 073

L

Leaves
- Balancing Nature, 063
- Branch Weaving, 031
- Creating Mandalas, 044
- Funny Nature Faces, 048
- Leaf Reliefs, 038
- Milk Jug Bird Feeder, 051
- Natural Loose Parts, 060
- Nature Artistry, 043
- Nature or Not?, 027
- Nature Reading Nooks, 074
- Painted Leaves, 039
- Shake a Shrub, 003
- Sorting Bonanza, 061
- Texture Walk, 007
- Treasure Tubs, 026
- Tree Cookie Weaving, 032
- Using Natural Dyes for Ink, 073
- Writing With Nature, 072

M

Moss
- Natural Loose Parts, 060
- Nature Artistry, 043
- Pond Jars, 002
- Treasure Tubs, 026
- Using Natural Dyes for Ink, 073

Mud *(see Dirt)*

P

Pebbles *(see Rocks)*

Pinecones
- Balancing Nature, 063
- Branch Weaving, 031
- Creating Mandalas, 044
- Discovering Pinecones, 011
- Funny Nature Faces, 048
- Natural Loose Parts, 060
- Nature Artistry, 043
- Nature or Not?, 027

Shake a Shrub, 003
Sorting Bonanza, 061
Treasure Tubs, 026
Tree Cookie Weaving, 032

Plants
- Air Plants, 087
- Aquaponics Fun, 023
- Cacti Curiosity, 086
- Container Gardens, 091
- Herb Hullabaloo, 010
- Hydroponic Garden, 094
- Indoor Water Gardens, 092
- Natural Loose Parts, 060
- Natural Sponge Garden, 093
- Nature Artistry, 043
- Nature's Spirals, 033
- Pond Jars, 002
- Sweet Potato Vines, 095
- Using Natural Dyes for Ink, 073
- Writing With Nature, 072

Pumpkins
- Funny Nature Faces, 048
- Natural Loose Parts, 060
- Playing With Pumpkins & Gourds, 025

R

Recipes
- Bark Sandwich, 040
- Basil Caterpillars, 100
- Cherry Tomato Jam, 099
- Chia Seed Pudding, 089
- Corntastic Soup, 019
- Dandelion Pancakes, 101
- Dandelion Soufflé, 101
- Dirt Dough, 041
- Frog on a Log, 013
- Green Smoothie, 100
- Ladybug Snacks, 012
- Making Mint Sun Tea, 010
- Modeling Sand, 042
- Pansy Pancakes, 059
- Pesto Posse, 100
- Pineapple Upside-Down Snack, 096
- Potpourri, 058
- Rainbow Fruit Skewers, 083
- Roasty Toasty Seeds, 025
- Seashell Clay, 079
- Stone Soup, 068
- Sunny Snacks, 085
- Very Berry Berries, 018
- Whoooo's Hungry?, 053

Rocks
- Alphabet Rock Game, 070
- Balancing Nature, 063
- Can You Estimate?, 071
- Creating Mandalas, 044
- Funny Nature Faces, 048
- I'm Here Today!, 069
- Musical Maracas, 045
- Natural Loose Parts, 060
- Nature Artistry, 043
- Nature Construction: Building in a Big Way!, 082
- Nature or Not?, 027
- Papier Mache, 054
- Rainbow Rocks, 067
- Rock Collections, 066
- Seashore Sand Inspection Center, 009
- Sorting Bonanza, 061
- Story Stones, 068
- Texture Walk, 007
- Treasure Tubs, 026
- Writing With Nature, 072

S

Sand
- Nature or Not?, 027
- Pond Jars, 002
- Sand Designs, 042
- Sand Sorting, 008
- Seashore Sand Inspection Center, 009
- Texture Walk, 007
- Treasure Tubs, 026

Seashells
- Alphabet Seashell Match, 080
- Balancing Nature, 063
- Can You Estimate?, 071
- Container Gardens, 091
- Creating Mandalas, 044
- Funny Nature Faces, 048
- Natural Loose Parts, 060
- Nature Artistry, 043
- Nature or Not?, 027
- Nature's Spirals, 033
- Papier Mache, 054
- Seashell Journaling, 081
- Seashells by the Seashore, 079
- Seashore Sand Inspection Center, 009
- Sorting Bonanza, 061
- Stringing Seashells, 046
- Treasure Tubs, 026
- Whimsical Mushroom Fairy Garden, 097

Seeds/Seed Pods
- Balancing Nature, 063
- Can You Estimate?, 071
- Charming Cherry Tomato, 099
- Container Gardens, 091
- Creating Mandalas, 044
- Exploring Sunny Sunflowers, 085
- Fascinating Pods, 088
- Funny Nature Faces, 048
- Growing Sunny Sunflowers, 084
- Musical Maracas, 045
- Natural Loose Parts, 060
- Natural Sponge Garden, 092
- Nature Artistry, 043
- Ok Okra!, 047
- Seeds Galore, 089

Shake a Shrub, 003
  Sorting Bonanza, 061
  The Grass is Always Greener, 098
  Treasure Tubs, 026
  Using Natural Dyes for Ink, 073
  Whimsical Mushroom Fairy Garden, 097
Sticks *(see Twigs)*
Stones *(see Rocks)*

T
Trees
  Bamboo Ladybug Feeder, 012
  Gourd Birdhouses, 052
  Maple Sugar Tapping, 004
  Milk Jug Bird Feeder, 051
  Natural Loose Parts, 060
  Nature Construction:
      Building in a Big Way!, 082
  Nature Reading Nooks, 074
  Pound Away, 078
  Shake A Shrub, 003
  Wood Drawer Ladybug Feeder, 012
  Woodblock Artistry, 034
  Writing With Nature, 072

Tree Cookie
  Balancing Nature, 063
  Creating Mandalas, 044
  Funny Nature Faces, 048
  Natural Loose Parts, 060
  Nature Construction:
      Building in a Big Way!, 082
  Pound Away, 078
  Tree Cookie Alphabet & Numerals, 077
  Tree Cookie Constructions, 075
  Tree Cookie Countdown, 076
  Tree Cookie Weaving, 032
  Woodblock Artistry, 034
  Writing With Nature, 072

Twigs
  Balancing Nature, 063
  Branch Weaving, 031
  Can You Estimate?, 071
  Creating Mandalas, 044
  Driftwood Discoveries, 017
  Funny Nature Faces, 048
  Geometree!, 065
  Milk Jug Bird Feeder, 051
  Natural Loose Parts, 060
  Nature Artistry, 043
  Nature Construction:
      Building in a Big Way!, 082
  Nature or Not?, 027
  Nature Reading Nooks, 074
  Not a Stick, 016
  Pond Jars, 002
  Shake a Shrub, 003
  Sorting Bonanza, 061
  Sticky Sticks, 037
  Treasure Tubs, 026
  Twig Easel, 036
  Twiggy Tic-Tac-Toe, 035
  Unit Sticks, 064
  Using Natural Dyes for Ink, 073
  Writing With Nature, 072

V
Vegetables
  Comparing Corn, 019
  Farmer's Market Fun, 100
  Kitchen Scrap Gardens, 096
  Painting With Kitchen Scraps, 049
  Seeds Galore, 089
  Sweet Potato Vines, 095
  Using Natural Dyes for Ink, 073
  Writing With Nature, 072

Credits

All photographs from *Shutterstock* except as follows: *Adobe Stock*—full page across from Introduction, full page across from 001, 002 grid (hand with reed), 003, full page across from 011, 015 grid (child with magnifying glass), 017, full page across from 018, 019 grid (hands holding corn), 026, 028 (small), second full page across from Creating, full page across from 035, full page across from 038, 040 grid (blue painted bark and birch bark), 041 (large), 045 (gourd), full spread after 049, full spread after 059, full spread after Thinking, 066 grid (child with rock), full page across from 069, 081, 083, 085 grid (hands with sunflower head), full spread after 088, 091 (ice cream cone plants), full page across from 097, 097 (large), full page across from 099, 099 grid (child eating tomato); *ISMILE Alam Atelier School*—030 grid (all photos), Conclusion, The Fish Journey, first grid (all photos except fish close-up), second grid (all photos), full page across from fish skeleton, third grid (all photos); *Jody Martin*—Dedication (Honor, Hope, Liberty, Roman, Shea, Waverly, and Wyatt), 037 (large), 043 grid (hand with shells in sand), 063, 065 (twig shapes on paper), full page across from 071, 079, 079 grid (child counting shells); *Nature's Way Preschool*—004 (large); *Sandra Duncan*—Dedication (Sierra), 002 grid (plant in jar and pond jars), 010, 015 grid (hand weaving web, beaded web, burlap web), 016 (sticks with yarn), 019 grid (markers in corn kernels), 025 grid (labeled gourd display, child with hammer, pumpkin with nails, child holding pumpkin, table and chairs), 029 grid (child with bowl, nature tray, corner tree), full spread before 030 (painting by Mala M. Peifer 3rd Grade), 030 (Fish Art by Renee Clyde), 031, 032, 033 grid (purple flower), 033 (Rolled Paper Bowl by Miller Students/collaborative project), 035 (large), 036, 038 (small), 039, full spread after 039, 040 (Painted Bark by Jeremiah), 041 (dirt dough), 043 grid (tree cookies on placemat and loose part construction), 044 (Mandala drawing by Iddings Students/collaborative project), full page across from 047 (Okra Mobile by Merrillville Students/collaborative project), 050 grid (bird resource center, Birds on Limb by Lauryn Leahy, Birds on Fence by Sam Russell, Fingerprint Birds by Kolling Students/collaborative project), 051, 055 (ceiling tile painting), 056 (painted bricks and cinderblock storage), 057 grid (pressed leaves and flowers), 060 grid (pinecone container and loose parts bowl), 061 grid (utensil tray, wooden container, and wicker basket), 061 (geometric container), 062, 064, full page across from 065, full page across from 068, 069, 072 (large), 074 grid (child in striped tent), 075 grid (checkers and scale), 076, 077, 078, 079 grid (seriated shells), 080, 082, full spread after 082, 091 grid (hat gardens and plant in shell), 091 (seedlings in red tray), 095, 096 grid (pineapple plant), 097 (small), 099 grid (painting and hands with tomatoes), 100 grid (peppers and summer squash), 101 grid (pressed flowers); *Taura Horn*—060 grid (children with loose parts), 075 grid (child stacking tree cookies); and *Tricia Turpenoff*—back cover author photo (Jody Martin). All illustrations by Kelsey Moline.

In Gratitude

Thank you to the following for their support and integral contributions to this book:

Anchorage Park, Barbara Shore, Bianca Woodberry, Blaine & Hannah Wheaton, Brandi Dietz, Child Development & Learning Laboratory of Central Michigan University, Cheryl Dickson, Children's Home + Aid, Gillian McAuliffe, Hagy Center for Young Children, Heather Parker Goetzinger, Irvine Nature Preschool, Isaiah Huppenthal, ISMILE Alam Atelier School, Jen Sticken, John Martin, Julie Ranalli, Kay Koern, Liberty O'Connor, Linda Wywialowski, Lycel Arboleda, Mary Clare Munger, Melanie Vega, Messiah Moravian Preschool, Milgard Child Development Center at Pierce College, Monique Heeg, Nature's Way Preschool, Dr. Padnya Patet, Region 16 Head Start, Ruth Wilson, Sally Fowler Haughey, Sharyl Robin, Sierra Elizabeth Austin, Summit School, The Adventure Club, Vicki Wright, and Waverly Schreiber.

On occasion, a collaboration brings together individuals that inspire each other to reach above and beyond, and results in an outcome that far exceeds expectations. Such was our creation process with the production team. The contributions that Stacy Hawthorne, Kaitlyn Nelsen, and Emily Rose have made to nurture our vision of this book into the resource you hold in your hands are truly remarkable. They infused our creation process with a joyful spirit and their passion for connecting children with nature. We are filled with gratitude for their commitment.

www.ingramcontent.com/pod-product-compliance
Lightning Source LLC
Chambersburg PA
CBHW061129010526
44117CB00023B/2998